Acquisition Guidelines No. 11

GUIDE TO Managing Approval Plans

WITHDRAWN

Susan Flood, Editor

ASSOCIATION FOR
LIBRARY COLLECTIONS
& TECHNICAL SERVICES

ACQUISITIONS SECTION
PUBLICATIONS COMMITTEE

AMERICAN LIBRARY ASSOCIATION
Chicago and London
1998

The editor wishes to thank the various members of the *Guides* Subcommittee of the ALCTS, Acquisitions Section, Publications Committee, who reviewed and commented on drafts of this *Guide* during 1995 and 1996. In particular, appreciation is extended to Starla Doescher and Nancy Slight-Gibney, the two leaders of the *Guides* Subcommittee who saw this work through its many revisions and who prodded and encouraged along the way. The three outside reviewers also made substantial contributions to the content and organization of this publication.

Composition by the dotted i in Times and Helvetica using QuarkXpress 3.32 for Macintosh 7600/132

Printed on 50-pound Victor Offset, a pH-neutral stock, and bound in 65-pound Vellum by Victor Graphics

The paper used in this publication meets the minimum requirements of American National Standard for Information Sciences—Permanence of Paper for Printed Library Materials, ANSI Z39.48-1992. ∞

Library of Congress Cataloging-in-Publication Data

Flood, Susan C.
    Guide to managing approval plans / Susan Flood.
        p.   cm. — (Acquisition guidelines ; no. 11)
    Includes bibliographical references and index.
    ISBN 0-8389-3481-1 (acid-free paper)
    1. Approval plans in library acquisitions—United States.
I. Title. II. Series: Acquisitions guidelines ; no. 11.
Z689.A2746 1973 no. 11
025.2—dc21

Copyright © 1998 by the American Library Association. All rights reserved except those which may be granted by Sections 107 and 108 of the Copyright Revision Act of 1976.

Printed in the United States of America.

02 01 00 99 98   5 4 3 2 1

Contents

I. Purpose and Scope   1

II. Introduction   1
   A. Definition and Types of Plans   1
   B. History   2
   C. Today's Approval Plans   3

III. Why Use Approval Plans?   3
   A. General Considerations   4
      1. Cost and staff issues   4
         a. Acquisitions   4
         b. Collection management   4
         c. Financial management   4
      2. Selection and returns   4
         a. Acquisitions   4
         b. Collection management   5
         c. Financial management   5
      3. Comprehensive coverage   6
         a. Acquisitions   6
         b. Collection management   6
         c. Financial management   6
   B. Special Applications   6
      1. Public libraries   6
      2. Foreign language plans   7
      3. Specialized areas   7

IV. Vendor Selection   7
   A. Vendor Identification   8
      1. Domestic vendors   8
      2. Foreign vendors   8
   B. Vendor Evaluation   9

- C. The Total Package   11
    1. Machine-readable invoice data   11
    2. Pre-processing   11
    3. Management reports   12
    4. Notification forms   12
    5. Vendor contacts   13

V. The Final Agreement   13

VI. The Profile   14
- A. Profile Definition   14
    1. Communication   14
    2. Structure   14
- B. Profile Preparation   15
    1. The people   15
        a. Faculty, librarians, and staff   15
        b. Vendor   16
    2. Preparation   16
        a. Examine profile structure   16
        b. Select subject coverage   16
        c. Budget for plan   16
        d. Define expectations   16
    3. Books vs. notification   17
    4. Standing orders   17

VII. Implementation of the Plan   17
- A. Acquisitions Processing   17
    1. Workflow   17
    2. Space   18
    3. Duplicates   18
    4. Returns   19
- B. Retrospective Collection Development   19
- C. Financial Management   20

VIII. Vendor Review   20

IX. Refining the Plan   21
- A. Collection Management   21
    1. Monitoring coverage   21
        a. Profiles   21
        b. Presses   22
    2. Returns   22
        a. Ten-percent benchmark   22
        b. Coding of titles   23

    B. Financial Management   23
        1. Marginal material   23
        2. Foreign plans   23

X. Future Applications   24

Appendix—Sample Profiles   27

Notes   45

Glossary   48

Selected Bibliography   53

Index   57

I. Purpose and Scope

The purpose of this *Guide* is to provide an introduction to approval plan management. For more information about approval plans, other sources, such as Cargill and Alley's *Practical Approval Plan Management,* are referenced in the bibliography. This *Guide* includes a discussion of considerations in the implementation of an approval plan, strategies for the management and supervision of a plan once it is in place, some definitions of terms associated with approval plans, a short bibliography of sources that expand on the topics covered here, and some sample approval plan profiles. The intention is to provide a useful guide for those who have little or no experience with the approval plan concept—students in master's programs in library or information science, administrators who are considering an approval plan to save staff time or optimize the book budget, neophytes in collection management or acquisitions, and those more experienced librarians who may be charged with rethinking or reworking an existing plan.

II. Introduction

A. Definition and Types of Plans

Approval plans are collection management and book acquisition tools. A vendor, together with collection management and acquisitions librarians, formulates a set of written, machine-readable guidelines or a *profile* that is analogous to a collection development policy. The profile can be subject-based, publisher-based, based on country of origin or the type of material, or profiles can be developed that combine all of these elements. A common type of plan is the subject-based plan, which can cover any number of the subjects found in library materials. Non-subject parameters evaluate titles on the basis of characteristics other than subject, such as academic or scholarship level, price, language, physical format, country of origin, and series or textual treatment (e.g., textbooks, anthologies, picture books, directories, proceedings, or computer programs). Once a profile is established and an agreement is reached on the discount and invoicing and shipping arrangements, the library will begin to receive books automatically. The vendor will run the library's profile against a batch of new titles, usually weekly, and ship those titles which match to the library. It is not necessary for the library to order title by title. Titles that are not considered appropriate may be returned.

Another common plan is one used for foreign titles that employs vendors for publications in each country or for each language that the library wishes to collect. The plan can be further defined by subject, by author, or by publisher. Other types include publisher plans, especially for university presses. Approval plans have also been developed based on type of material, such as music scores, art exhibition catalogs, children's titles, non-print media and best-sellers. These can be further defined by non-subject parameters, but typically there are fewer specified parameters on these types of plans than on subject-based plans. The library may not feel the need to critically review receipts for these other types of approval plans because the criteria for selection are usually much more clear-cut than for subject-based plans.

B. History

The approval concept is not a new one. Documentation exists which indicates that the concept was used in the latter half of the nineteenth century.[1] (Refer to the glossary for descriptions of approval-type plans which predate the type discussed in this *Guide,* such as blanket orders, Farmington Plan, gathering plans, Greenaway Plan, Latin American Cooperative Acquisition Project, and PL-480.)

Approval plans, as we now know them, were conceived by Richard Abel in the early 1960s.[2] Abel observed that book budgets were growing faster than personnel budgets and that a core group of publishers produced the majority of scholarly titles. Before the 1950s librarians often ordered directly from publishers and received little or no discount from them.[3] The lengthy process of identifying titles for purchase and then ordering, receiving, and processing them meant that often eighteen months to two years passed after publication before a book was available to a library patron. Richard Abel realized that computers held the key to efficiency. His book company added a service dimension to its wholesaling business when it matched the profiles from all its library customers to titles that had been coded for content and then sent huge orders to the publishers. Because he ordered in such large quantities, he could negotiate large discounts from the publishers and pass on some of the savings to the libraries. The books initially came to libraries with preprinted bibliographic forms and later with cataloging records that reduced the library's processing costs. His sales force marketed the plan to (1) reduce the delay in the acquisition of books, (2) reduce the library's processing costs, and (3) systematize collection development for the new programs that were being started at many colleges.[4]

C. Today's Approval Plans

The major reason that the approval concept has endured is that these plans are a cost-effective method for the acquisition of library materials. The vendor identifies titles before they are published through such means as pre-publication orders from publisher representatives, publisher catalogs, and advance copies. The vendor codes the titles, orders and receives them. A computer matches the coded titles with the library's profile. Titles that match are shipped to the library and those that do not are excluded. Materials arrive at the library's site, are reviewed and either accepted or rejected. First the vendor and then the library make selection decisions. A close working relationship between vendor and librarian is required for the plan to be effective.

Approval plans fill a need for the library materials themselves and for value-added services such as notification of new titles, bibliographic and authority records, and shelf-ready books. When a library chooses this latter option, which includes spine labels and bar codes, the plan becomes a blanket order, rather than an approval plan, because vendors cannot offer highly processed books for resale and do not permit returns. The library may also request special shipping and billing accommodations and load invoices electronically into its automated accounting system.

Developments in approval plans have been driven by changes in automation and the economic climate. Rising costs, especially for serials, have reduced funds available for library materials. The continuing expansion of information and the downsizing of the library staff are additional economic factors. Approval plans will continue to evolve as competition forces companies to reevaluate traditional and shrinking product lines and develop new markets.

III. Why Use Approval Plans?

While librarians in collection management or acquisitions may initiate exploration of instituting an approval plan, the decision to actually proceed with a plan should be made by a group representing collection management, acquisitions, and cataloging.

A. General Considerations

1. *Cost and staff issues.* The Association of Research Libraries SPEC Kit 141, published in 1988, lists staff savings as the most common reason for adopting an approval plan.[5] These savings are evident in acquisitions, collection management, and financial management.

    a. *Acquisitions:* In acquisitions, approval plans reduce the amount of pre-order searching or verification, order preparation, or filing of purchase orders. The time spent in processing approval receipts is much less than the time that would be spent on the same titles ordered through a traditional order process.

    b. *Collection management:* In collection management, approval plans reduce the time librarians must spend scanning book reviews, bibliographies, and publisher catalogs. Selectors are able to focus on material that is not covered by the approval plan—unique and difficult-to-find titles, local materials, ephemera, foreign titles, new serials, videos and CD-ROMs—and rely on the approval plan to acquire titles which are relatively easy to identify.[6]

    c. *Financial management:* Approval plans consolidate billing with a few vendors. The financial manager may use one allocation instead of dozens of internal funds. In this case, the accountability of charging receipts to specific areas is relinquished in return for ease in processing. Bookkeeping may be simplified if a library chooses not to use encumbrances for each title that it receives. Invoicing can be processed electronically. A library may also choose to establish a deposit account with a vendor, thereby in effect prepaying in exchange for a discount that may range from 1.5 percent to 4.5 percent more than a regular plan. Some institutions place constraints on prepayment, but if this method of payment is allowed the vendor will send titles until the prepaid amount is exhausted. With this arrangement, checks do not have to be cut for each batch of invoices.

    As greater compatibility develops between the book vendors' automated systems and the integrated library system vendors, the potential savings will increase. As libraries and booksellers move forward with X12 and EDI (electronic formats for business transactions), a unique interface will no longer be necessary for every type of electronic data interchange. Standardization will simplify electronic transactions between libraries, vendors, and publishers with a concurrent reduction in costs.

2. *Selection and returns*

    a. *Acquisitions:* Both the library and the vendor hope to minimize returns, but if returns are necessary approval plans offer the advantage of streamlined procedures for processing unwanted titles. Any titles which are judged to be unacceptable may be returned without authorization from the vendor, although titles must still be packaged for return and records kept of rejected titles and eligible credits.

b. *Collection management:* An approval plan offers an advantage in that selection can be made with book in hand. Before a title reaches the library, the vendor codes it with book in hand. The vendor then responds to library needs as outlined in the profile. The library reviews the book upon receipt. Inspection may reveal good reasons for buying a title that are not readily apparent from a citation.

This method of acquisition is not without its critics. An approval vendor assumes a greater responsibility for meeting a library's collection management objectives than does a vendor who only fills firm order requests. Such an arrangement presents unique challenges for both librarians and vendors. With the adoption of an approval plan, collection management librarians may sense a loss of control. Teaching faculty may view with suspicion attempts to divert a portion of the usual funding toward purchases or a program they may not understand. The criticism has been leveled that the vendor is concerned with sending the most profitable titles, not necessarily the best quality titles, in order to deliver at the discount expected by the library.[7] Or, stated another way, "Approval plan vendors work best with large, established publishers and are able to provide approval service at discounted prices because of the cost effectiveness generated by economies of scale."[8] Resentment on the part of faculty and selectors as expressed in terms of "turning over collection development to a businessman" is alleviated if all parties are accommodated and involved in the implementation of the plan. The collection management expertise that was formally directed toward the selection of individual titles must now be centered on the drafting of the library's profile. If a good collection development policy is in place at the outset, communication with the vendor and the profiling process will be facilitated. For their part, vendor employees must operate in a business environment, but they also must be able to relate to their library customers. Vendors can increase satisfaction with approval plans if book coders and sales representatives are people with library experience. Communication between the vendor and library personnel in collection management and acquisitions determines the success or failure of the approval plan.

c. *Financial management:* The approval agreement may call for either the library or the vendor to pay the shipping cost for returns. Some vendors allow the library to simply deduct the charge for the returned title from the invoice total; others may require credit memos for returns. These credit memos are initiated by the library and do not need the vendor's prior permission.

3. *Comprehensive coverage*

   a. *Acquisitions:* Through the use of approval plans, books are acquired before they become subject to inflationary increases or go out of print. Timely acquisition has assumed greater importance since a 1979 court decision involving the *Thor Power Tool Company.* In that case, the IRS successfully challenged accounting methods used for inventory and publishers, like other businesses, responded with smaller inventories. The result is that smaller print runs have increased the number of out-of-print and out-of-stock notices that libraries receive. Approval plans allow the library to take advantage of the competitive pricing of first print runs. Timely acquisition means that the title is available at the lowest cost as soon after publication as possible.

   Approval plans are a way to receive a large number of titles quickly. When they are in place, titles are often available to scholars and students when they have need of them. Patrons do not have to wait while the request is ordered, received, and processed.

   b. *Collection management:* Another advantage of approval plans is that they help develop orderly, balanced collections and counter the tendency of faculty with highly specialized research programs to build collections that only support personal interests. Even a profile that is restricted to notification via forms or slips, as opposed to book coverage, has been shown to broaden selection.[9]

   c. *Financial management:* If the budget is so limited that it cannot support the commitment that a plan requires, then an approval plan is not an option. An approval vendor may offer some management tools to help counter budget difficulties which could force mid-year suspension of ordering. The vendors are able to produce analyses of publishing output by cost and volume of publication. These analyses, in addition to library-specific management reports, allow a library to anticipate inflation, monitor the budget, and make profile adjustments early in the fiscal year.

B. Special Applications

   1. *Public libraries.* Most discussions of approval plans in the library literature focus on applications in academic libraries. One article does, however, address the use of approval plans in a public library setting.

The emphasis in Judy Quinn's "The New Approval Plans: Surrendering to the Vendor . . . or in the Driver's Seat?" is on the use of approval vendors for opening day collections, retrospective collection development, and book lists created from vendor's databases.[10] It also discusses some of the advantages and disadvantages of an approval plan for a public library. On the plus side, she lists staff savings, better discounts, efficiency, help with foreign-language materials, and timely acquisition of titles before they go out of print. Vendors are able to set profiles so that libraries will receive award winners or popular titles. On the minus side, she mentions the problem created by titles that the vendors miss. Specifically, she refers to the publishers of reference books whose titles must be ordered directly and are not available through a vendor.

Those public libraries that prefer to review titles with book in hand find approval plans attractive. Book-in-hand review seems particularly important for children's literature. After review, orders are placed for multiple copies. Often public libraries receive preview copies from major publishers, but approval plans help them identify titles from smaller publishers that might otherwise be missed. Public libraries that use approval plans must also have the financial resources to support this continuing obligation.

2. *Foreign language plans.* Approval plans can be used for the acquisition of foreign materials as well. Some foreign materials go out of print quickly; so, it is important to acquire them as soon after publication as possible. Many vendors are country-specific. Others use bookstores in a group of countries to create a regional list. A good vendor can assure timely acquisition of foreign titles.

3. *Specialized areas.* Approval plans have been developed based on type of material, such as music scores, art exhibition catalogs, children's titles, best-sellers and non-print media. These plans may be variously defined by language, author, publisher or source, age level or time period, price, binding, or format, but typically there is not as great an array of specifications for these types of plans as there is for subject-based plans. The criteria for selection are usually more clear-cut than for subject-based plans.

IV. Vendor Selection

The selection of an approval vendor is extremely important. Today's complex approval plans make the task of choosing and switching vendors challenging. Libraries demand customized plans and vendors who can meet their unique needs. Once established, it is not easy to give up this relationship in order to change to another vendor, one reason being that profile instructions do not transfer easily from vendor to vendor because the terms, logic, and construction of vendors' profiles may not resemble each other. If a vendor has assumed cataloging functions as well as acquisition functions, a change of vendors becomes even more complex.

A. Vendor Identification

1. *Domestic vendors.* The number of prospective domestic vendors is not large. The book trade has seen takeovers, buy-outs, and mergers in recent years, and approval vendors have not been immune to this trend. The acquisitions manager or the committee charged with vendor selection will want to examine the promotional literature that approval vendors distribute. Phone calls or electronic mail requests to libraries that have plans will be the next step.

2. *Foreign vendors.* Vendors for foreign materials can be identified through requests posted in electronic resources such as ACQNET or ACQWEB, through browsing the World Wide Web, through visits to the exhibit area at library meetings, and through conversations with librarians at institutions who have experience with the acquisition of foreign publications. Another resource is the volumes of an Association for Library Collections and Technical Services publication entitled *Foreign Book and Serial Vendors Directories.*[11] (As of the writing of this *Guide,* the volumes *Book and Serial Vendors for Asia and the Pacific* and *Book and Serial Vendors for Africa and the Middle East* have been published and are also available electronically from ALA.) A good vendor can assure timely acquisition of foreign titles.

    One problem that is unique to British approval plans is that many or most titles that are of interest to U.S. libraries are eventually published here. At least one vendor presently offers to supply the cheapest available edition whether it is from the United States or the United Kingdom. Anthony Ferguson studied this issue in an article in *Collection Building* in 1988.[12] In 1991 Betsy Kruger found that 80 percent to 90 percent of the titles of more than local interest were eventually published in the United States, most within three months of their initial publication in the United Kingdom.[13] The study by Mary Eldredge in 1994 updated this research and found that 27 percent of the U.K. titles were not subsequently published in the United States.[14] Often the U.S. edition is cheaper. (The price differential is also analyzed in these articles.) Is your library willing to wait, or is it important to have the titles as soon after publication as possible? Another consideration is the availability and acceptability of cataloging copy for editions from the United Kingdom. A title received in a timely manner is of no use if it is held on arrival to await cataloging. Perhaps the breadth of coverage offered by a British vendor is enough justification to proceed with a British plan. Librarians must not only compare the packages offered by the various British approval vendors, but they must also compare these offerings with the service from a U.S. vendor.

B. Vendor Evaluation

There have been several significant articles that outline methodology for the evaluation of vendors.

Through questioning, librarians can obtain an impression of how well the vendor covers the subjects assigned. Joan Grant, in *Understanding the Business of Library Acquisitions,* lists questions to pose to other libraries during the vendor selection process and to use later for vendor evaluation.[15] Her questions touch on the adequacy of the profile; selectivity and coverage; the list of publishers covered by the plan; the cost in terms of discount, shipping charges, and returns; the usefulness of slips or forms coverage; the information contained in the vendor's management reports; the helpfulness of the sales and customer service representatives; and finally the ease of processing shipments. The vendor must be committed to quality and train its staff to pay attention to detail. Grant's questions and others can help match the vendor to the library.

A classic series of three articles on vendor selection and evaluation was published by Reidelbach and Shirk in the journal *Library Acquisitions: Practice & Theory* in the 1980s. Although specific references are dated, the ten steps in the initial article remain valid today. Reidelbach and Shirk discuss (1) developing a preliminary approval plan design; (2) identifying potential vendors; (3) questions for eliciting vendor information; (4) evaluating vendor information; (5) planning on-site visits; (6) gathering reactions from those attending visits; (7) checking with other libraries; (8) re-evaluating the information; (9) notifying vendors of the results; (10) scheduling of the profile session.[16]

A more recent article in *Library Acquisitions Practice & Theory* by Frances Wilkinson and Connie Thorson outlines how the RFP process can be used to select a vendor.[17] Using the RFP process allows librarians to judge vendors on all aspects of their operations, not just discount and service charges. Wilkinson's and Thorson's article details specifics on the number and type of RFPs, the time line, the committee, on-site presentations, the writing process, selection criteria, and response evaluation. An interview with Gary Shirk of Yankee Book Peddler in Wilkinson's and Thorson's article also spells out what the library should provide the vendor in order to respond to an RFP—"(1) size and rate of expenditure; (2) composition of expected purchases; (3) realistic performance expectations: (4) preferred payment options, e.g., acceptability of deposits; (5) pricing expectations; (6) realistic view of what is most important to the library; (7) willingness to balance a number of factors in the decision; (8) ability to renegotiate if unexpected circumstances occur; (9) names of decision makers; (10) details of the decision making process; (11) RFP process schedule; site visit requirements and sufficient lead time; (12) openness of libraries to new vendors; (13) if more than one vendor award is possible, then specific scope of the possible awards."[18]

Some other details follow that should be considered in the vendor interview.

- During the interviews with prospective vendors, the library will want to ask the vendor if it can provide reports on the titles that would have been received if the plan had been in place for a given period of time, on the average price per book per subject, and a one-year cost projection based on the proposed profile. These reports will give the library an idea of the scope of the plan.
- Invoicing should be discussed. Some libraries use a batch invoice with a lump sum for the total shipment. Other libraries want a title-by-title invoice using slips or sheets with the titles listed in alphabetical order.
- The discount rate and how the discount rate could be improved with a deposit account should be negotiated. (A deposit account will generally increase the discount from 1.5 percent to 4.5 percent.) A regular discount is often uniform throughout the invoice and does not apply the optimum amount for each title. Libraries may not realize any great savings in discount over their firm orders.
- The starting date of the plan and its duration should be negotiated.
- The method and schedule of deliveries should be established. What carrier will be used? Are there any special shipping charges? How should the shipping labels be addressed? Approval plans for foreign material pose special problems. Delivery may not be as prompt or as certain as domestic plans, although air freight to a U.S. port and then surface mail to the library will speed delivery and keep costs lower than the cost of air freight to deliver directly to the library.
- The library needs to determine who will pay the shipping charges on returns. Will the library write its own credit memos or simply deduct the returned title from the invoice total?
- Finally, the bibliographic forms that come with the books should be examined. Even libraries that use integrated systems may find these forms useful as a record of receipt in an order file, a processing slip, a record of titles included in an invoice payment, part of the paperwork to be returned with a rejected title or a new-title alert for personnel in public services or faculty in academic institutions.

C. The Total Package

Interestingly, typical acquisitions concerns such as discount and speed of delivery are often not the determining factors in vendor selection; rather, selection is determined by the total package of vendor services. Vendors are developing value-added services which require an increasing investment in technology. The data processing staff that vendors employ has also grown steadily.[19] Many vendors offer online access to their databases for title, availability, and specific client/profile match information. Some libraries also use their online access to read reviews or the table of contents of new publications. A library should expect to pay for these services and the following through reduced discounts or as a separate charge:

1. *Machine-readable invoice data.* Machine readable or electronic invoices may be an option for some libraries. The invoice data output must meet client specifications. Even if the vendor's invoice data are not electronically compatible with the library's accounting system, a locally designed system can sometimes use the data the vendor supplies with its machine-readable bibliographic records for the library's own financial records.

2. *Pre-processing.* Perhaps the most important auxiliary service that the approval vendor can supply is the provision of machine-readable acquisitions records or full bibliographic or authority records for transfer to the library's online public catalog. Some libraries prefer using acquisitions records to create their own copy. Others purchase authority control from their approval vendors. Still others prefer to use full MARC/CIP records. This kind of outsourcing has blurred the lines between cataloging and acquisitions and brought a fundamental change and challenge to the way libraries organize their work. Personnel have to be trained to identify when a bibliographic record is acceptable and when it is not. Judging what elements of the bibliographic record are crucial can only be accomplished when there is close cooperation between cataloging and acquisitions.

   The extent to which vendor-supplied records must be reviewed is also a joint decision. Will the library accept Canadian (CANMARC) or United Kingdom (UKM) records? Member copy? Are CIP records acceptable or will the library want to pay a vendor to upgrade them or choose to upgrade them locally? Should acquisitions personnel sort receipts depending on the record source or encoding level?

   Vendors and bibliographic utilities have developed cooperative relationships that provide bibliographic records and automatically establish holdings of library ownership in national databases. Bar codes have been added to vendor pre-processing services which include spine labels, inside call number labels, date due slips, security targets, and property stamps. The decision to receive shelf-ready approval books or even titles that have been processed through a bibliographic utility is a management decision that should be based on a clear understanding of anticipated outcomes of such a decision:

- Does the library hope to achieve a reduction in costs or time savings?
- What are the current costs and how do they compare with the vendor's prices for these services?
- Will vendor pre-processing release staff to perform other services or take on special projects?
- Is the goal better products or services?

A detailed discussion on outsourcing is beyond the scope of this booklet on approval plans. A library that is interested in a high degree of outsourcing will choose a vendor who is efficient in moving material through all of the special services and who has a number of customers to share the costs of support for these services.

3. *Management reports.* Other auxiliary services that are part of the total vendor package include the customized management reports for the local library and the general reports analyzing the data from all of the titles that the vendor has processed. Examples of the management reports should be examined to make sure that they can be used to do cost projecting and monitoring. The cost analysis by subject may not fit a particular institution's definition of those subjects. A customized management report can also be requested which lists titles shipped by subject or publisher. Reports that analyze claims, selections from the notification service, and returns may also be provided. On request the vendor may provide budgetary projections analyzing the impact of any profile changes being contemplated.

4. *Notification forms.* During the course of processing approval titles, machine-generated information is produced by the vendor which is then used either on a bibliographic form or as a notification slip. The bibliographic forms are used by vendors' employees to "pick" the books from inventory shelves that are sent to libraries pursuant to their book plans and accompany the titles to the libraries. This same information can also generate announcements of newly published titles—either printed on slips or forms or sent in electronic format—instead of the shipment of the material itself. Although not technically an approval plan, the library may opt to receive only notification with the option to order and receive the material on a title-by-title basis.

The format for this current awareness service for new titles can be paper or electronic. The library should expect evaluative information on the form. Does the library understand all of the codes? Samples should be inspected. Is the format complete? The paper version has one title per form and can be sorted and distributed to subject specialists. A large number of forms may require some time to sort and distribute. The electronic version can be mounted on a local area network for use by subject specialists.

Vendors expect that the titles sent to the library through this service will create business for the vendor who produced the list of titles, not a competitor. Is there a discount on orders generated by the new titles service? What procedures should be used to place these orders? If the discount or service is undesirable on orders generated from these lists, the discount or service should be negotiated or another vendor should be found to supply notification of new titles.

Just as a library uses a profile, review, management reports, and a budget to control the expenditures for material actually shipped on approval, so also do expenditures generated by forms need to have controls. If forms are used to create firm orders, then encumbrances which commit funds for form purchases are in place. The method of charging specific approval funds for forms also allows the library to separate the basic approval costs from form purchases which may be in subject areas outside of the core program. It is also advisable to enter records for form purchases into the library's acquisitions system. Otherwise, manual files must be checked before placing a firm order.

5. *Vendor contacts.* As with any good firm order vendor, an approval vendor's relationship with publishers puts the vendor in a position to pass on news of mergers, bankruptcies, new imprints, etc., to customers and to negotiate discounts and other services from publishers. The library depends on the vendor to maintain steady relations with all of the publishers to be covered by the plan to ensure that no titles are missed. A vendor which is dependent on one person for these contacts is in danger of missing titles, if the essential person is suddenly no longer with the company.

V. The Final Agreement

When the library is finally ready to select a vendor for its approval plans, the institution's requirements must be followed. Is there a bid requirement? Is a written contract necessary? A verbal agreement may be all that is necessary, but it is still good advice to have a letter of intent with a list of specifications.

Samples of invitations to bid, letters of intent, and specifications are included in Cargill and Alley's *Practical Approval Plan Management*.[20] Those librarians wishing to use the RFP process should consult Wilkinson and Thorson's article in *Library Acquisitions: Practice & Theory*.[21]

If the vendor is providing machine-readable acquisition records or cataloging copy or electronic invoices, arrangements have to be made for the data transfer. Machine-readable bibliographic records may come in the form of magnetic tape, diskette, or file transfer protocol. Will the records come before or after the shipment of books? How often will they come? How should they be addressed? Will there be a charge? What format will be used for the invoices? What elements must be present on the invoices? These and other questions concerning data transfer must be addressed.

VI. The Profile

A. Profile Definition

1. *Communication.* All who have a stake in the ultimate outcome of the approval plan—collection management, acquisitions, and the vendor—need to be involved in profile definition. A satisfactory profile requires the cooperation of all. The profile translates the library's needs to the vendor. It is the embodiment of the collection development policy, whether written or understood, and can be used to communicate that policy to faculty, students, or administrators. Its creation is time-consuming for both the library and the vendor. Once in place, it does not become a static entity. Rather, it is often in a constant state of refinement as needs and budgets change.

2. *Structure.* Most U.S. vendors have developed unique profile structures to accommodate elaborate combinations of subjects and non-subject modifiers to target specific collection management objectives. In countries outside of Europe, profiles may not be as sophisticated as those of domestic vendors. Even a cursory examination of the sample profiles included in the appendix of this publication reveals the wide variety offered by vendors' profiling systems. In basic terms, either a vendor's approval thesaurus will follow the Library of Congress classification schedule or its own classification system. It is not the intent here to analyze the impact this difference has. What is basic to most of the profiles is that non-subject parameters modify subject areas. Even though elaborate profile combinations are possible, a good case can be made for simplicity to improve predictability of receipts and reduce the margin of error. For this reason, some would argue for a simpler publisher-

based plan for domestic titles, instead of a subject-based plan. Others argue that mergers and takeovers have made even publisher-based plans unpredictable.

Some vendors offer profiles with 5,000 or more subject descriptors and non-subject modifiers. Non-subject modifiers include (1) type of publisher, (2) country of origin (3) language of publication, (4) format, (5) treatment of text, (6) academic level, (7) inclusion in a series or continuation, (8) price.

The thesaurus of subjects is arranged hierarchically by LC classification or by a vendor-developed order. This arrangement allows the library to choose all or part of a subject.

Some common non-subject modifiers that libraries use to exclude materials from coverage are reprints, titles accompanied by multimedia, government publications, dissertations, periodicals, textbooks, juvenile books, and popular or mass-market publications.

The library can opt to have multiple profiles with different non-subject modifiers for different parts of the collection. Or, the library may want to vary the treatment of titles from different publishers through the use of non-subject modifiers (e.g., collect all university press publications but only those titles appropriate for undergraduates from commercial publishers).

With some vendors the library can also specify a preference for hardbacks or paperbacks and a price differential that triggers the shipment of the paper over the hardcover edition. Or, it can order paper bindings and ask the vendor to rebind before shipping and billing. Or, the paperbacks can be bound by the library's own bindery. With this option the library must be willing to trade a processing delay for savings in its book budget.[22]

B. Profile Preparation

The chapter by Dana Alessi in *Issues in Acquisitions: Programs and Evaluation* and Robert Nardini's article "The Approval Plan Profiling Session" in *Library Acquisitions: Practice & Theory* expand on the profile preparation process.[23] The following comments are meant only as some general observations.

1. *The people*
    a. *Faculty, librarians, and staff:* The first step to a successful profile is to identify those staff—professional and support—who will either be involved with the vendor visit to create the profile or who will set up other arrangements, such as those for shipping and billing. The profiling visit may include all selectors and in addition may include

representatives of the library's accounting staff. The group should not be unwieldy, but no one should feel left out. The acquisitions librarian, the head of collection management, or a committee could be in charge.

b. *Vendor:* The vendor should be apprised of the schedule of meetings in advance of the date set for the vendor visit. The visit may begin with a general session, break into groups of related areas or interdisciplinary studies, and then follow with meetings with individuals. It is also helpful if the vendor is provided with a list of names of those involved and an idea of the library's organizational structure.

2. *Preparation*

   a. *Examine profile structure:* Library personnel should examine a vendor's profiling system to become familiar with the structural organization of the subjects and the non-subject parameters. Profile structure varies widely from vendor to vendor. Although an analysis of the underlying characteristics of and differences between the major vendors' profiling schemes is beyond the scope of this *Guide,* an appendix of sample profiles is provided for examination. In addition to the profile, a report from the vendor of title output by subject and the resulting cost per subject should be received ahead of the visit.

   b. *Select subject coverage:* Preliminary discussions might be held to discuss what material should be covered by the approval plan. Issues that could be discussed include default non-subject modifiers and whether or not non-subject modifiers should remain the same for all profiles. The collection development policy should be reviewed. If selectors support the policy, the library has gone a long way toward a successful profile.

   c. *Budget for plan:* Decisions should be made on the amount of money to set aside for approval and how it is to be allocated. If the money is not allocated in one fund, procedures need to be established to handle departmental allocations and expenditures.

   d. *Define expectations:* Once the vendor arrives, discussions will cover these issues again. In academic libraries, it is useful to have a copy of the curriculum available and information about enrollment and intervals between the same course offerings. The profile may be used to cover the core curriculum. On the other hand, the subject bibliographers may be doing an excellent job in the basic areas, but they may need some help in areas outside of their expertise, such as titles in an unfamiliar language or unique specialization. Some publishers and subject areas cannot be supplied, and these need to be identified. The library should discuss its expectations for coverage of societal publishers who often require prepayment, offer no discount, and accept no returns.

3. *Books vs. notification.* The profiling session will include not only decisions with regard to the books the library wishes to receive but also decisions with regard to the notification it wishes to receive on new titles published outside of its book profile. Notification could be in paper format or in an electronic version delivered via magnetic tape, diskette, or FTP file. The pros and cons of book coverage versus simple notification of new titles that are published should be weighed. The library may opt to begin the profile with notification only. Libraries also may choose coverage with notification rather than with the automatic shipment of titles, when there has been a problem with an inordinate number of returns. Some foreign vendors provide coverage only by forms or slips. If the titles received through this service are inappropriate, then the profile should be changed.

4. *Standing orders.* During the visit or shortly after it, the vendor will want to receive a current and complete list of library standing orders for monographic series, sets, annuals, and continuations. This list should be maintained with continuations added as orders are placed. These titles will be blocked on the approval plan to prevent duplication. If no list is provided, the profile should cover the various continuation types with bibliographic announcements rather than with the automatic shipment of material. Alternatively, standing orders could be canceled with the intent of letting the profile dictate what titles are sent. Some would argue that this method ensures receipt of only those titles that meet collection management objectives, instead of all titles that happen to be assigned to the same series title.[24]

VII. Implementation of the Plan

A. Acquisitions Processing

1. *Workflow.* The work in acquisitions shifts from ordering to receiving. This shift requires a redesign of workflow. Bibliographic records are entered at point of receipt. In some libraries, downloading of bibliographic records also includes attaching the library's holdings symbol to the title in the database of a national bibliographic utility. Procedures have to be developed to remove these holdings for titles that are dupli-

cates or that are rejected and returned. Supervisors should examine the workflow to reduce labor-intensive exceptions to procedures.[25]

2. *Space.* Space is required to display the new arrivals for a review by collection management professionals to ensure that receipts are meeting the library's needs. In those libraries where subject specialists review titles, a typical display is for one week with the titles grouped by subject. Acquisitions staff screen for duplication or error. Acquisitions personnel may need to format a checklist to track the review process. Titles are reviewed by selectors for appropriateness and quality and cost criteria. Selectors may also be responsible for assigning a fund and location for the title and may question acquisitions personnel about the rationale for the shipment of an individual title. The answer should be determined by examining the codes assigned to the book, the vendor's thesaurus, and the library's profile.

If the approval plan is working well with returns in the range of 1 percent, a library may decide that the cost benefit of review does not justify the time and effort necessary to sort and arrange titles by subject, review them, and then re-sort them in invoice order at the end of the display period.[26] In this case, no review space is required. In those libraries where only one person is responsible for review, space requirements may be minimal because titles may not need to be sorted by subject and may not have to remain on display for a fixed period.

3. *Duplicates.* Approval plans also require changes in firm order procedures to prevent duplication of firm ordered titles on the approval plan. Some libraries may have a separate staff for the approval and firm order units. Other libraries may have personnel shift back and forth or have one person handling it all. A profile which limits coverage to the major publishers simplifies determination of what will be treated on the approval plan. To avoid duplication, firm orders must be held awaiting receipt on approval or profiles and vendors' databases must be checked before placing the order. Access to the information in vendors' databases has eased the problem of not knowing which titles will come on the approval plan and such databases may be mounted locally and updated regularly by the vendor, or they can be accessed via the Internet. The use of workstations facilitates simultaneous use of a bibliographic utility, the library's system, and a vendor's database. Microfiche records, while not as current, can also be used to determine what the library will receive. These tools are valuable aids to discovering whether or not a title will be treated on the plan and, if so, whether the library will receive it. Some vendors will fill firm orders before they send out their approval shipments and sometimes a library may be shorted when

a title is shipped because the vendor does not have enough copies for all customers. These titles should be claimed.

The library staff should establish a policy on whether to order a book immediately or wait for the approval copy. If the staff decide to hold an order in anticipation of receipt on approval, they may load a record in the online catalog with a date set to prompt a claim in case the book does not arrive when expected. If two copies are received, the approval copy may be returned, but it is usually better for the library to accept both copies and then to dispose of the duplicate through established means, e.g., through a book sale or as an added copy in another location. The copy received through a firm order and the copy sent on the approval plan were both supplied by the vendors because of instructions sent from the library. Likewise, an approval copy that duplicates a gift was sent in response to instructions defined in the profile and should be retained if it is at all possible.

Placing firm orders, standing orders, and approval orders with one vendor can reduce the amount of duplication. Otherwise, titles in series on standing order must be blocked on approval by the series title. Lists of standing orders must be sent to the approval vendor and this list should be maintained. If it is possible to place a firm order with the instruction "do not duplicate on approval," then the library can place firm orders with confidence that the title will not also come on approval.

Some libraries use more than one approval vendor. If more than one vendor is used and the division is by subject, overlapping subject areas may create problems with duplicate shipments of the same title.

4. *Returns.* Many public libraries choose not to return titles received on approval for a number of reasons: if there are no returns, the discount is improved; the review process is often too lengthy to allow for returns; and it is easier to offer the title for sale through a Friends of the Library organization than it is to process the return.

For foreign plans, returns are more expensive. In countries where cost and profit margins are low, selection tools weak, and conventional orders do not work, it does not make sense to return large numbers of books. In this case, returns only hurt the library and the vendor.

B. Retrospective Collection Development

The vendor's database may also be used to generate lists for retrospective collection development. The search strategy can be simple—works by a specific author or titles from a particular press—or complex, utilizing many of the available profiling parameters to generate lists of titles which are in print or which must be searched through out-of-print sources. A tape in standardized format of the library's holdings can be run against the vendor's files.[27] Vendors can also use statistical analyses of selected peer libraries to provide start-up collections for new institutions.

C. Financial Management

There are variations in approval spending because of publishing seasons but calculations are fairly accurate in predicting whether or not approval spending is on target. The profile or other spending can be adjusted to respond to inflation or a reduced budget with the goal of a steady stream of expenditures throughout the fiscal year.

VIII. Vendor Review

Some of the same processes mentioned in Joan Grant's chapter in *Understanding the Business of Library Acquisitions* and in the article by Wilkinson and Thorson to evaluate and then select an initial vendor for the library's approval plan can also be used to periodically review vendors' performance.[28] Periodic review assists the library in evaluating whether or not a vendor's service is satisfactory, whether or not optimum use has been made of the library's resources, and whether or not another vendor might better serve the library's needs. During the review, collection management and acquisitions personnel will have the opportunity to communicate their objectives to each other and to the potential vendors. The library should be prepared to give a minimum of one month's notice for the termination of a domestic plan or a three-month notice for a foreign plan.

One method of vendor review involves comparing two slip plans or comparing an existing book plan with another vendor's slip plan. One of the problems with such a comparison is that it is difficult to devise instructions that result in competitors doing exactly the same thing. Another difficulty is timing the study so that both vendors are treating the same pool of titles. One vendor might have treated several important titles before the study began.

The library can also identify titles through its regular selection methods and highlight those it would expect to come on approval. This list can be checked against those titles that are treated on approval. This method of comparison will give the library a sense of the percentage of titles that could have been selected through traditional means that would actually come on the approval plan. It will not give the library a sense of the number of titles that would have come on approval that traditional selection methods would not have identified.

A more systematic plan for vendor review is outlined in an article by Womack, Adams, Johnson, and Walter published in 1988.[29] What follows is a summary of their plan:

1. Development of the Approval Plan Vendor Review Checklist
2. Contacting and scheduling prospective approval plan vendors
3. Development of evaluation procedures to be used by library staff participating in the vendor review
4. Providing instructions to staff participating in the vendor review
5. On-site vendor presentations
6. Analysis of the Evaluation Form
7. Initial deliberations and recommendations
8. Conducting telephone reference checks with other libraries
9. Discount negotiations.

Further information on vendor review can be found in the sources listed in Beau David Chase's "Approval Plan Evaluation Studies: A Selected Annotated Bibliography, 1969–1996."[30]

IX. Refining the Plan

A. Collection Management

1. *Monitoring coverage*

    a. *Profiles:* Profiles are flexible instruments. Subject areas or non-subject parameters can be added or deleted with budget or curricular changes. Collection management librarians should plan to review profiles at regular intervals for continuing relevance to changing programs. Budget changes may dictate a change in price limitations. In lean years the profile can be adjusted to reduce receipts, but programs can also be run to generate lists of titles for purchase to make up for past deficiencies. Given enough lead time, changes in the profile will help the library prepare basic collections for any new emphasis in the curriculum, new faculty, or new degree programs. Library staffing must be adequate to spend the time required to evaluate the plan in view of changing circumstances and to communicate changing needs to the vendor. Circulation statistics, feedback from users, statistical analyses that compare peer institutions and time/effort/concern from collection management can all be used to evaluate the plan. Library administrators should be prepared to commit adequate resources to the plan for it to be successful. Perhaps specified intervals for review should be established to ensure that every profile is reexamined in light of changing personnel and politics.

Libraries with limited budgets who are trying to cover finely defined areas with highly specialized non-subject parameters may not find approval plans successful.[31] One other special problem that bears mentioning is the difficulty in acquiring scientific and technical material via an approval plan. This problem is addressed in the article by Glorianna St. Clair and Jane Treadwell.[32] A large part of scientific literature is published outside of the major commercial companies. Publications of societies and associations are much more difficult for an approval vendor to track than titles produced by the major publishers because they often change editorship and location. Careful monitoring is especially important in these specialized areas.

   b. *Presses:* As presses emerge, libraries can recommend that they be added to the approval plan list of publishers. Vendors will usually accommodate this request if the discount offered by the publisher is competitive, return terms are reasonable, at least five titles a year are anticipated, and the press will sell on approval. Vendors need advance advertising and a commitment to publish.[33] Likewise, a press may be deleted if the emphasis of its title list changes.

2. *Returns*

   a. *Ten-percent benchmark:* If receipts do not match expectations or if the library is returning more than 10 percent of receipts, collection management personnel and vendors should examine the profiles and management reports to determine the cause. Management reports detail the quantity of returns within broad subject areas and also may tabulate the reasons for returns. For particularly difficult problems, acquisitions personnel may want to temporarily create their own database for return information. The information from these reports should help to modify the profiles to reduce the return percentage. Perhaps a new selector or a change in criteria is causing returns to increase. A newly established plan may experience a higher rate of return. Sometimes, however, the profile as designed by the vendor is constructed so that fine adjustments are not possible. The acceptable percentage of returns may be even lower than 10 percent if the books come with a high level of pre-processing. Libraries that choose to receive books that are already processed often give up the right to return. If the return rate is unacceptable, new titles in these troublesome subjects may be covered best through a paper or electronic notification service instead of coverage that prompts the automatic shipment of books.

    b. *Coding of titles:* Unhappiness with receipts may be caused by the vendor codes assigned to the title, rather than the functioning of the profile. Vendors typically code books twice. Using agency gathering plans and publisher announcements, the vendor enters data into its automated systems. The preliminary codings are created in advance of the appearance of the finished product. A second examination occurs with book in hand. Generally, only those titles which match after the second examination are shipped. After the initial coding, orders are generated to publishers by matching the titles with all of the libraries' profiles. The coding process is much like classification. Sometimes the vendor's coding does not match the way a title is classified by a library selector. Dissatisfaction with the way a book is coded is often a source of unhappiness with how a plan functions.

B. Financial Management

1. *Marginal material.* Two observations may be made here. On the one hand, there is a tendency to retain marginal material that comes via approval. Libraries need to remember that there are processing and housing costs associated with the retention of marginal material in addition to expenditures from the book budget. A commitment to the plan will help ensure that staff and time limitations do not create a work environment that makes acceptance of titles far easier than critical selection. On the other hand, faculty tend to reject more titles than do librarians because their interests generally are not as broad. Thus, faculty reviewers may contribute to a high return rate.

2. *Foreign plans.* It is difficult to estimate the cost of foreign plans. In many cases libraries have left the vendor to define the coverage—a stance that may or may not work, depending on the vendor and the budget. The prices of foreign titles also fluctuate with the exchange rate, shipping costs must be factored into the total package, and the discount is often less than for U.S. material or nonexistent. Libraries have a responsibility to keep the vendor informed of stringent budget limitations. For their part, vendors sometimes offer plans to mollify wide fluctuations in exchange rates caused by unstable monetary markets. Distance compounds any problems that may occur; therefore, the commitment to service that the vendor of foreign materials supports is especially important.

X. Future Applications

What does the future hold? In the short term, vendors will continue to develop value-added services that will help them gain a larger share of the library market and librarians will make greater use of technology to enhance approval plan processing. These services include fund accounting, electronic claiming, original cataloging, and authority control. When a library chooses a high level of pre-processing, such as shelf-ready books, titles can no longer be sent "on approval" and the plans become blanket orders. As budgets shrink, libraries will continue to search for ways to do more with less. Martin Warzala writes that economics will force academic libraries away from using the approval concept for the acquisition of books.[34] Instead, academic libraries will apply the concept to the acquisition of information, packaged in other ways than as a book. Approval plans will be used to acquire media such as audio, video, CD-ROMs, and interactive media. The approval concept will also be extended to information acquired through document delivery and databases. Warzala believes that the use of approval plans for books in public libraries, however, will continue to increase.

Databases that have been developed for approval customers will be available for broader uses and appropriate charges will be levied to support their enhancement. Customers will search their vendors' databases using the library's online system as the user interface. Libraries presently notify vendors when they find errors of omission in vendor's databases so that all customers will benefit. This monitoring may become more organized than it is now. Libraries in a regional group or consortium may reach a point at which each member agrees to cover a particular subject or group of publishers and monitor the accuracy of the database for its assigned area. Vendors will be able to support automatic, coordinated collection development through the use of interfaced profiles for regional groups or consortia. All of these features and more will be made possible by standard electronic formats and records that facilitate communication and reduce the need for human intervention.

Profile functions will reside on local systems so that maintenance can be done at home. Profiling will become more automated and incorporate characteristics of faculty, students, and circulation patterns into profile construction. Widespread use of expert systems or something similar to predict approval plan receipts has the potential of preventing firm orders for titles that will come on approval.[35] Although many vendors try to accommodate firm orders tagged "do not duplicate on approval," libraries will pressure them to enhance and refine this service. Some vendors presently send pre-publication announcement forms that allow selectors to cancel the status of a title in the vendor's database.[36] In the future library system personnel may even download records to the library's OPAC to show what is on order through the approval plan. Libraries could then authorize titles before they are sent. Ultimately, firm orders and titles slated to come on approval could have holdings pre-set on a bibliographic utility, such as OCLC, which may help prevent libraries from firm-ordering a duplicate copy. The advantages of such an enhancement of bibliographic records in a national utility would have to be weighed against the disadvantage for interlibrary loan requests of holdings data set for items the library does not yet own or may reject.

Deficiencies in approval coverage of small presses, societies, institutes, proceedings and simple title omissions by the larger vendors can contribute to library collections that resemble each other.[37] (This assumption has been challenged in a study by Robert F. Nardini, Charles M. Getchell Jr. and Thomas Cheever in *The Acquisitions Librarian*.[38]) The acquisition of foreign language materials and other unique titles may suffer if too large a percentage of resources goes to domestic approval plans. It is unique selections by subject bibliographers who create the differences between collections. Sharply decreased budgets for materials and collection management personnel, as well as careful scrutiny of order requests in light of projected use, probably have more to do with this trend than the use of approval plans, but together they may be making the task of securing unique titles through interlibrary loan or through a photocopy of the original more and more difficult.

Libraries and vendors will continue to cooperate to develop the means to acquire information. Changes will continue to be driven by the marketplace, and librarians will continue to seek creative solutions as they struggle with fewer resources and greater demands.

Appendix—Sample Profiles

Note: These profiles are not intended to be used as a basis of comparison, but only as an indication of the variety of plans that are available. They are not totally representative of all vendors or all available plans. Included below is a list of URL addresses for the vendors. Many of these sites also contain sample approval plans.

Academic Book Center, Inc.
  http://www.acbc.com

Aux Amateurs de Livres
  URL unavailable

Baker & Taylor Company
  http://www.baker-taylor.com

Blackwell North America, Inc.
  http://www.blackwell.com

John Coutts Library Services
  http://www.coutts-ls.com

Harrassowitz
  http://www.harrassowitz.de

Ingram Library Services, Inc.
  http://www.ingrambook.com

Majors Scientific Books, Inc.
  http://www.majors.com

Midwest Library Service
  http://www.midwestls.com

Yankee Book Peddler, Inc.
  http://www.ybp.com

A. Academic Book Center, Inc.

Academic Book Center, Inc.
Approval Profile   FRNK - Subprofile Information (01   )

SUBJECT COVERAGE: Books

LC Classification	LC Description	Notes
A0001-QA0075	General Works General Works	
QA0077-QA0077	Science Mathematics	
SB0001-TT0999	Agriculture Plant Culture	
U0000-ZZZ9999	Military Science Military Science	

SUBJECT COVERAGE: Forms

LC Classification	LC Description	Notes
QA0076-QA0076	Science Mathematics	
R0000-RZZ9999	Medicine Medicine (Gen'l)	
S0001-S0954	Agriculture Agriculture	
TX0000-TXZ9999	Technology Home Economics	

NON-SUBJECT PARAMETERS

DESCRIPTION	ACTION	NOTES
PRICE LIMITATION:	$100	
GENERAL READERSHIP LEVEL		
GRADUATE	BOOK	
LAYPERSON	BOOK	
PROFESSIONAL	BOOK	
UNDERGRADUATE	BOOK	
NON-SUBJECT PARAMETERS:		
ANTHOLOGY	BOOK	
ATLAS	BOOK	
BIBLIOGRAPHY	BOOK	
CLINICAL/MEDICAL	FORM	
COMPUTER BK (GEN'L: HIGH LEVEL)	BOOK	
COMPUTER BK (GEN'L: LOW LEVEL)	FORM	
COMPUTER BK (LANGUAGE-SPECIFIC)	FORM	
COMPUTER BK (MODEL-SPECIFIC)	FORM	
COMPUTER BK (W/SOFTWARE DISK)	FORM	
COOKBOOK	FORM	
DICTIONARY / THESAURUS	FORM	
ENCYCLOPEDIC WORK	FORM	
FICTION, POETRY, PLAY	BOOK	
GENERAL POPULAR TREATMENT	BOOK	
HANDBOOK	FORM	
HOW-TO BOOK: FOR LAYPERSON	FORM	
NON-STANDARD BINDING	FORM	
PRACTITIONER TREATMENT	FORM	
PROGRAMMED TEXT/WORKBOOK	FORM	
REGIONAL LOCAL INTEREST	FORM	
REPRINT	FORM	
SERIOUS TRADE TREATMENT	BOOK	
TEXTBOOK, GRADUATE	FORM	
TEXTBOOK, UNDERGRADUATE	FORM	
USER MANUAL	FORM	

B. John Coutts Library Services

```
JOHN COUTTS LIBRARY SERVI                              TYPE:  E
COUTTS SUBJECT CODE SELECTION TABLE - AUTOMATIC CUSTOMER
         SUBJ CODE   DESCRIPTION                    1 2 3 4 5

         151510      Canadian Drama                 Y Y Y
         151520      Canadian Essays                Y Y Y
         151530      Canadian Fiction               Y Y Y
         151545      Canadian Literary Criticism    Y Y Y
         151560      Canadian Poetry                Y Y Y
         151570      Canadian Satire/Humor          Y Y Y
         352        Business Studies               Y Y
         352050      Accounting                     Y Y
         352055      Management                     Y Y
         352055510   Advertising                    Y Y
         352055530   Executive Management           Y Y
         352055065   Operations Research            Y Y
         352055085   Project Management             Y Y
         352055540   Financial Management           Y Y
         352055560   Marketing/Sales                Y Y
         352055570   Personnel Management           Y Y
         352055580   Production Management          Y Y
         352055065   Research and Development       Y Y
         352055590   Public Relations               Y Y
         352075      Office Practice                Y Y
         352075555   Office Communication           Y Y
         352075560   Office Equipment               Y Y
         352075085   Word Processors                Y Y
         353        Economics                      Y Y
         353510      Economic History and Conditio  Y Y
         353515      Economic Theory                Y Y
         353515550   Macroeconomics                 Y Y
         353515555   Microeconomics                 Y Y
         353520      Finance                        Y Y
         353522015   Banking                        Y Y
         353522025   Insurance                      Y Y
         353522030   Investment                     Y Y
         353522065   Public Finance                 Y Y
         3535220654C Taxation                       Y Y
         353525      Industry                       Y Y
         353525510   Agricultural Economics         Y Y
         353525520   Co-operatives                  Y Y
         353525530   Energy Economics               Y Y
         353525535   Entrepreneurship               Y Y
         353525560   Production Economics           Y Y
         353525560030 Industries and Trades         Y Y
         353525570   Small Businesses-Economics     Y Y
         353530      International Economics        Y Y
         353535055   Development Studies            Y Y
         353540      Labor Economics                Y Y
         353540055   Industrial Relations           Y Y
         353540556G  Trade Unions                   Y Y
         353540070   Labor Market                   Y Y
         353560      Land Economics                 Y Y
```

29

C. Ingram Library Services, Inc.

Advance Buyer's Checklist (ABC)

Advance Buyer's Checklist is designed to give you the flexibility and control necessary to tailor new title selections to the tastes of your community. We take our knowledge of author track records, publisher, timeliness of topic, publisher's promotion and advertising budget, print run, and author tours—factors which influence patron demand—and use them to create a list of suggested titles for your library.

Every month we send you a report summarizing the titles reserved for your account in that month. You review the report and make any changes—increase quantities, cancel titles, etc. You return the report to us and we prepare your shipment. Most importantly, Ingram reserves inventory to fill your ABC order. Your book will arrive soon after release, in the quantities you need. ABC is a convenient, flexible way to help you select new titles.

C. Ingram Library Services, Inc. (Continued)

Sample Grid

HARDCOVER

IF INGRAM ORDER QUANTITY IS SEND ME THIS QTY. OF EACH NEW PUBLICATION		H 1-24	G 25-49	F 50-99	E 100-149	D 150-299	C 300-999	B 1,000-4,999	5,000+
Animals	AN								
Antiques/Collectibles	AO								
Art & Architecture	AR								
Automotive	AU								
Bibles	BI								
Biography/Autobiography	BA	1	1	2	2	3			
Business/Economics/Finance	BE						3	3	
Children's Books/Baby-Preschool	CH								
Children's Books/Ages 4-8	CI								
Children's Books/Ages 9-12	CJ			1	1	1	1	1	
Children's Books/Young Adult	CK								
Children's Books/All Ages	CL								
Computers, Communication	XE					1	1	1	
Computers, General	XG					1	1	1	
Cooking/Wine	CW					1	1	1	

INGRAM - BOOKSELLER'S FIRST CHOICE

HARDCOVER

IF INGRAM ORDER QUANTITY IS SEND ME THIS QTY. OF EACH NEW PUBLICATION		H 1-24	G 25-49	F 50-99	E 100-149	D 150-299	C 300-999	B 1,000-4,999	5,000+
Medical/Nursing	PI								
Nature/Guide Books	NA						1	1	1
New Age/Occult	OP								
Nonfiction-Crime/True Adventure	NC						1	1	
Nonfiction-General	NF								
Performing Arts	PA								
Philosophy	PH								
Photography	AP		1	1			1	1	1
Poetry/Plays	PO						1	1	
Politics/Current Events	PL								
Pop Arts	PR	1	1	1			1	1	1
Psychology/Pop Psychology/Counseling	PS								
Recovery	HE						1	1	
Reference	RB		1	1			1	1	1
Religion-Biblical Studies	RF							1	

Please remember to enter a quantity for each level code (H through A) as is shown in the sample grid. For example, if you wanted one copy of everything Ingram ordered in excess of 300 in category X, you would need to place a "1" in each corresponding square C through A.

D. Midwest Library Service

MIDWEST LIBRARY SERVICE APPROVAL PROGRAM PROFILE

Profile for: 90328-601 SAMPLE PROFILE   Date: 8/26/96

B A F S N   *   *   *   L C CLASSIFICATION OUTLINE   *   *   *

		N	J-JX		POLITICAL SCIENCE
		N	J		General legislative and executive papers
		N		1-9	Official gazettes
		N		10-87	United States documents
		N		80-85	Presidents' messages and other executive documents
		N		86-87	State documents
		N		100-981	Other documents
		N	JA		Collections and general works
		N	JC		Political theory. Theory of the state
		N		311-323	Nationalism
		N		325-341	Nature, entity, concept of the state
		N		345-347	Symbolism, emblems of the state: Arms, flag, seal, etc.
		N		348-497	Forms of the state
		N		501-628	Purpose, functions, and relations of the state
		N		571-628	The state and individual. Individual rights. Liberty
	F		JF		Constitutional history and administration
	F			8-2112	General works. Comparative works
	F			201-723	Organs and functions of government
	F			751-786	Federal and state relations
	F			800-1191	Political rights and guaranties
	F			1321-2112	Government. Administration
	F			2011-2112	Political parties
		N	JK-JQ		Special countries
	F		JK		United States
		N		2403-9501	State government
		N		9661-9993	Confederate States of America
	F		JL		British America. Latin America
	F		JN		Europe
	F		JQ		Asia. Africa. Australia. Oceania
		N	JS		Local government
		N		141-231	Municipal government
		N		241-285	Local government other than municipal
		N		301-1583	United States
	F		JV		Colonies and colonization. Emigration and immigration
B			JX		International law. International relations
B				63-1195	Collections. Documents. Cases
B				101-115	Diplomatic relations (Universal collections)
B				120-191	Treaties (Universal collections)
B				1305-1598	International relations. Foreign relations
B				1625-1896	Diplomacy. The diplomatic service
B				1901-1995	International arbitration. World peace. International organization
B				2001-5810	International law (Treaties and monographs)

B - Books within profile, A - Books profile override (blanket coverage),
F - Forms within profile, S - Forms profile override (blanket coverage), N - Nothing

D. Midwest Library Service (Continued)

MIDWEST LIBRARY SERVICE APPROVAL PROGRAM PROFILE

Profile for: 90328-601 SAMPLE PROFILE   Date: 8/26/96

B A F S N   *   *   *   L C CLASSIFICATION OUTLINE   *   *   *

```
          N   K-KWX              Law
B             K                     Law (General)
B                    201-487           Jurisprudence. Philosophy and theory of law
B                    520-5582          Comparative law. International uniform law
B                    7000-7720         Conflict of laws
          N   KD-KDK              Law of the United Kingdom and Ireland
B             KD                     England and Wales
    F                8850-9312            Local laws of England
          N          9320-9355            Local laws of Wales
          N          9400-9500            Wales
    F         KDC                     Scotland
    F         KDE                     Northern Ireland
    F         KDG                     Isle of Man. Channel Islands
    F         KDK                     Ireland (Eire)
B             KDZ                  America. North America
B                    1100-1199           Organization of American States
          N   KE-KEZ              Law of Canada
B             KE                     Federal law. Common and collective provincial law
          N   KEA-KEZ                Individual provinces and territories
          N   KEA                       Alberta
          N   KEB                       British Columbia
          N   KEM                       Manitoba
          N   KEN    0-599              New Brunswick
          N          1200-1799           Newfoundland
          N          5400-5999           Northwest Territories
          N          7400-7999           Nova Scotia
    F         KEO                       Ontario
          N   KEP                       Prince Edward Island
          N   KEQ                       Quebec
          N   KES                       Saskatchewan
          N   KEY                       Yukon Territory
          N   KEZ                       Individual cities, A-Z
B             KF-KFZ              Law of the United States
B             KF                     Federal law. Common and collective state law
    F         KFA-KFW                Individual states
    F         KFA    0-599              Alabama
    F                1200-1799           Alaska
    F                2400-2999           Arizona
    F                3600-4199           Arkansas
    F         KFC    0-1199             California
    F                1800-2399           Colorado
    F                3600-4199           Connecticut
    F         KFD    0-599              Delaware
    F                1200-1799           District of Columbia
    F         KFF                       Florida
```

B - Books within profile, A - Books profile override (blanket coverage),
F - Forms within profile, S - Forms profile override (blanket coverage), N - Nothing

E. Yankee Book Peddler, Inc.

SAMPLE UNIVERSITY LIBRARY
YBP APPROVAL PLAN PROFILE (rev. 12/96)

B   Q   Science

See subject exceptions below.

NON-SUBJECT PARAMETER EXCEPTIONS:

Send books, all class Q, regardless of subject restrictions below, for:
HISTORICAL, BIOGRAPHICAL, MEDIEVAL, CLASSICS, PHILOSOPHICAL, ETHICAL ASPECTS OF SCIENCE.

ADVANCED-UNDERGRADUATE AND GRADUATE-LEVEL TEXTBOOKS.

Send notification slips, all class Q, for:

CONTEMPORARY SOCIAL ASPECTS OF SCIENCE; CULTURAL ASPECTS; POLITICAL, PUBLIC POLICY, ECONOMIC, BUSINESS ASPECTS;

COLLECTIONS OF PREVIOUSLY PUBLISHED ARTICLES; SINGLE AUTHOR COLLECTIONS, READERS; CONFERENCE PROCEEDINGS; PROGRAMMED TEXTBOOKS; UNREVISED DISSERTATIONS; ABRIDGMENTS; WORKBOOKS, EXAM QUESTIONS; DICTIONARIES; but do not restrict multi-language dictionaries.

S   Q   Science (General)

Send books for:

Q124-143 HISTORY OF SCIENCE.

Q174-175 PHILOSOPHY OF SCIENCE.

Q222-2995 SCIENTIFIC COMMUNICATION, ILLUSTRATION.

Send books for (Q, cont.):

Q300-387 ARTIFICIAL INTELLIGENCE, INFORMATION THEORY, KNOWLEDGE REPRESENTATION, ETC.

S   QA   Mathematics

Send books for:

QA8-10 PHILOSOPHY OF MATHEMATICS; MATHEMATICAL LOGIC.

QA21-29 HISTORY OF MATHEMATICS.

QA75-76 COMPUTER SCIENCE, IF RESEARCH OR THEORY-BASED; send notification slips for all guidebooks, i.e. practical titles intended for users of particular hardware, software, systems, languages, etc.

Send books in QA for (cont.):

QA150-295 STATISTICS, SEQUENCES; STOCHASTIC PROCESSES; PROBABLILITIES; ALGEBRA, LIE ALGEBRAS; MACHINE THEORY, GAME THEORY.

E. Yankee Book Peddler, Inc. (Continued)

SAMPLE UNIVERSITY LIBRARY
YBP APPROVAL PLAN PROFILE (rev. 12/96)

FORMAT:

- _B_ Biography/Autobiography
- _X_ Classroom Anthology
- _S_ Coffee Table Book
- _S_ Collected Works
- _S_ Collection (one author)
- _S_ Collection/Anthology (previously published material)
- _B_ Collection (new material)
- _B_ Conference Monograph
- _B_ Conference Proceeding
- _X_ Cookbook
- _B_ Correspondence
- _X_ Curriculum Guide
- _B_ Diary
- _X_ Exam questions
- _S_ Festschriften
- _S_ Grammar
- _X_ Hymn Book
- _S_ Lab Manual
- _S_ Museum Publication
- _S_ Music Score
- _S_ Periodical Anthology
- _S_ Personal Narrative
- _X_ Programmed text
- _X_ Textbook—introductory undergraduate
- _S_ Textbook—advanced undergraduate
- _S_ Textbook—graduate
- _S_ Textbook—professional
- _S_ Travel Guide
- _X_ Unrevised dissertation
- _X_ Workbook

IMPRINT:

- _B_ US
- _B_ UK
- _S_ Australia
- _B_ Canada
- _B_ Germany
- _B_ Netherlands
- _S_ India
- _S_ China
- _S_ Hong Kong
- _S_ Singapore
- _S_ Japan
- _S_ Other

CONTENT LEVEL:

- _X_ Juvenile
- _X_ Popular
- _B_ General Academic
- _B_ Advanced Academic
- _B_ Professional

LANGUAGE:

- _B_ English
- _S_ Other

NEW EDITIONS:

- _B_ New Edition
- _B_ Critical Edition
- _X_ Abridgment
- _S_ Supplement

NON-BOOK FORMATS:

- _B_ Book/Diskette
- _S_ Book/Audio
- _B_ Book/Fiche
- _S_ Diskette
- _S_ Audio Cassette
- _S_ Audio CD
- _S_ Video
- _S_ CD-ROM
  Exclude all which are not IBM-PC compatible
- _X_ Maps
- _X_ Oddity

PAGINATION

- _S_ Less than 50

PRICE CEILING:

Notification slips will be sent for titles above the following list price:

$255

REPRINTS:

- _S_ Reprint
- _S_ Facsimile
- _X_ Journal Monograph (single issue)

REFERENCE BOOKS:

- _B_ Handbook
- _B_ Dictionary
- _B_ Biographical Dictionary
- _B_ Dictionary/Multi-language
- _S_ Atlas
- _X_ Medical Atlas
- _B_ Bibliography
- _B_ Discography
- _B_ Filmography
- _B_ Bio-bibliography
- _B_ Directory
- _B_ Encyclopedia
- _B_ Concordance
- _B_ Index
- _B_ Thesaurus

SETS AND SERIES:

- _S_ Numbered series
- _B_ Unnumbered series
- _S_ Numbered sets-in-progress
- _B_ Unnumbered sets-in-progress
- _S_ Annuals
- _S_ Dated lecture series
- _S_ Non-monographic series
- _B_ Volume 1 of any continuation type

SIZE:

- _B_ Undersized

TRANSLATIONS:

- _B_ Translations into English
- _X_ Translations from English

F. Baker & Taylor Company

THE APPROVAL PROGRAM
     BAKER & TAYLOR CO.

WOMENS STDS

ATTN. ATTN: SAMPLE PROFILE

BOOK QUANTITY   1   PRICE LIMIT $100.00 S

MODIFICATION PATTERN FOR PUBLISHERS AND SUBJECTS WHICH FOLLOW

- - BOOK - -		- - SLIP - -		- - - EXCLUSIONS - - -	
PUBLISHER		PLACE OF PUB		TEXTUAL FORMAT	
COMMERCIAL	A01	FOREIGN, OTHER	B05	COMPUTER APPLCTN	H01
UNIVERSITY PRESS	A02	LANG OF PUB		PROG MATERIALS	H09
UNIVERSITY AFFIL.	A03	FRENCH	C02	ACADEMIC LEVEL	
SOCIETIES & ASSN.	A04	SPANISH	C03	COMM COL/ASSOC	I06
PLACE OF PUB		OTHER FOREIGN	C04		
UNITED STATES	B01	EDITIONS			
CANADA	B02	REPRINT	D04		
GREAT BRITAIN	B03	PHYSICAL FORMAT			
EUROPE	B04	SPIRAL	E03		
LANG OF PUB		LOOSELEAF	E04		
ENGLISH	C01	MULTI-MEDIA	E05		
EDITIONS		PAMPHLET	E06		
FIRST	D01	SUBJECT DEVEL			
SUBSEQUENT	D02	TECHNIQUES	G06		
TRANSLATION	D03	ACADEMIC LEVEL			
PHYSICAL FORMAT		EXTRA-CURRICULAR	I05		
HARDBOUND	E01	GEOGRAPH DESGN			
PAPERBOUND	E02	OCEANIA	J11		
CONTINUATIONS		LOCAL EMPHASIS	J13		
MONO SER 1ST ONLY	F01				

MODIFICATION PATTERN FOR PUBLISHERS AND SUBJECTS WHICH FOLLOW

```
    - - - BOOK - - -              - - - SLIP - - -              - - - EXCLUSIONS - - -
GEOGRAPH DESGN
  AFRICA              J09
  FAR EAST            J10
  NOT RELEVANT        J99
```

*** EXCLUDE SPECIFIED CONTINUATION TITLES ***

```
                                                 CODING      INFORMATION ....
                                            A02560000    5/  4/94     1
                                            A07114800    5/  4/94    21
                                            A08771000    5/  4/94     3
                                            A09164600    5/  4/94    35
                                            A11522000    5/  4/94    13
                                            A14662000    5/  4/94    12
                                            A14663000    5/  4/94    27
                                            A14664000    5/  4/94    25
                                            A14664040    5/  4/94    30
                                            A14664042    5/  4/94    29
                                            A14664050    5/  4/94    28
                                            A16760000    5/  4/94    18
                                            A23284600    5/  4/94    22
                                            A25100000    5/  4/94    16
                                            A25120000    5/  4/94    24
                                            A26100000    5/  4/94    17
                                            A31604800    5/  4/94    11
                                            A31604846    5/  4/94    15
                                            A34360800    5/  4/94    34
                                            A37100000    5/  4/94    33
                                            A41704800    5/  4/94     2

BOOK FOR ALL PUBLISHERS
  C    WOMEN AND ART
  PN   WOMEN IN PERFORMING ARTS
  ML   WOMEN AND MUSIC
  GV   WOMEN AND SPORTS
  BF   PSYCHOLOGY OF WOMEN
  D    WOMEN - ANCIENT HISTORY
  D    WOMEN - MEDIEVAL HISTORY
  D    WOMEN - MODERN HISTORY
  D    WOMEN - 18TH CENTURY HISTORY
  D    WOMEN - 19TH CENTURY HISTORY
  D    WOMEN - 20TH CENTURY HISTORY
  E    WOMEN IN THE U.S.
  PN   WOMEN IN LITERATURE
  PR   WOMEN AS AUTHORS (ENGLISH LITERATURE)
  PR   WOMEN IN ENGLISH LITERATURE
  PS   WOMEN AS AUTHORS (AMERICAN LITERATURE)
  HQ   SOCIOLOGY OF WOMEN
  HQ   FEMINISM
  HE   WOMEN IN BROADCASTING
  LC   WOMEN IN EDUCATION
  HQ   WOMEN AND POLITICS

                                                 CODING      INFORMATION ....
                                            A44302000    5/  4/94    19
                                            A48404226    5/  4/94    31
                                            A50504800    5/  4/94    20
                                            A66205042    5/  4/94    14
                                            A80284320    5/  4/94    32
                                            C39304015    5/  4/94    26
                                            H37142000    5/  4/94    23
                                            N44302000    5/  4/94     4

BOOK FOR ALL PUBLISHERS
  U    WOMEN IN THE MILITARY
  HD   WOMEN IN MANAGEMENT
  Q    WOMEN IN SCIENCE
  RC   HEALTH SERVICES FOR WOMEN
  T    WOMEN IN ENGINEERING
  HV   WOMEN IN POLICE WORK
  LC   WOMEN IN HIGHER EDUCATION
  V    WOMEN IN NAVAL SERVICE

                                                 CODING      INFORMATION ....
                                            A09204015    5/  4/94     5
                                            A13104800    5/  4/94     7
                                            A13321000    5/  4/94     6
                                            A13420500    5/  4/94     9
                                            A13461000    5/  4/94     8

SLIP FOR ALL PUBLISHERS
  GV   EXERCISE FOR WOMEN
  BL   WOMEN AND RELIGION (GENERAL)
  BL   WOMEN IN ASIAN RELIGIONS
  BM   WOMEN IN JUDAISM
  BP   WOMEN IN ISLAM
```

37

G. Blackwell North America, Inc.

```
BLACKWELL NORTH AMERICA, INC.    LIBRARY PROFILE FOR PRHI:K SAMPLE PROFILE

SUBPROFILE # 003    STARTING DATE 99-99-99    YEAR OF PUBLICATION 1996    BUY=N
SUBPROFILE DESCRIPTION: CHEMISTRY BOOKS

SUBJECT DESCRIPTORS:                                          # BFNOX

     48     Chemistry div                              01      X
   4810     Alchemy                                    01      N

PUBLISHERS:                        —BFNOX—

00001 ALL OTHER PUBLISHERS            X        57108 S Karger Publisher Inc
23790 J Cramer, GW                    F        47564 S Karger, SZ
66430 Parey, GW                       F        82635 Springer Vlg

NON-SUBJECT PARAMETERS:            —BFNO—

Academic difficulty level     01              Type of edition              06
  Lower undergrad textbook    03    N           Critical edition           01 B
  Upper undergrad textbook    04    N           Heavily illus book         06 B
  Graduate text               05    B           Original & translation     09 B
  Professional/practitioner   06    B           Translation                10 B
  University/research lib     08    B           General edition            11 B
  Undergraduate library       09    B           Photo collection           13 F
  Highly spec collection      10    B
  Popular collection          11    F        Language of book              07
                                                English                    01 B
Readership level              03                German                     02 F
  Specialist reader           01    B           Latin                      10 F
  Non-specialist reader       02    B           Spanish                    11 F
  General reader              03    F           French                     13 F
  Reference                   05    B           Italian                    14 F
                                                Modern Greek               17 F
```

NON-SUBJECT PARAMETERS: —BFNO—

Exam preparation	24	F
Pocket reference	26	F
Dissertation	29	B
Journal monograph	32	B
Musical score	34	N
Readings & cases	36	B
Hrdware/sftware specific	38	F
Documentary collection	39	B
Facsimile	41	B
Art exhibition cat	42	B

Polyglot	42	B
Any other language	44	B

Type of publisher   09

University press	01	F
Trade publisher	02	B
Societal	03	B
University/Univ dept	04	F
Small press	05	B
Govt publisher	06	B
Art museum	07	F
Personal author	08	B
Corporate body	09	B
Importer/distributor	13	B

LIST PRICE LIMITATIONS: —BFN—

List prices to $74.99   N   But not to exceed
But not to exceed $200.00   B   Greater than

16 Country of orig pub   17 Country of source pub

00001 All (other) countries		F
14000 Great Britain		N
41000 Canada		B
42000 United States		B

00001 All (other) countries		N
41000 Canada		B
42000 United States		B

SERIES NSP'S: —BFN—   —BFN—

19 1ST SERIES—1ST VOLUME   20 1ST SERIES—SUBS. VOL.

00001 All others in series	B

00001 All others in series		N
00003 Num monographic series		B
00005 Num monographic set		B
00011 Monographic conferences		B
00015 Editions		B
00017 Unnum monographic sets		B
00018 Unnum monographic series		B

H. Harrassowitz

HARRASSOWITZ

Approval Plan	Form Selection		
S	☒	13. History	See also Special Studies Areas: 04.03.0, 04.06.0 & 05.01.0-05.20.3
S	☒	13.01.0	History in General. ~~Reference Works & Bibliographies~~. Theory & Philosophy of History. Historic Methodology. Historiography. Study & Teaching of History. Organizations
☐	☒	13.02.0	General Auxiliary Sciences: Archives & Historical Records. Genealogy. Chronology. Numismatics. Epigraphy, etc. *For specific Auxiliary Sciences see individual countries below*
☐	☒	13.03.1	General History of Civilization & Culture. Universal History
C	☒	13.03.2	Jewish Diaspora (70-1948). Zionism
S	☒	13.04.1	General European History. ~~Reference Works & Bibliographies~~
S	☒	13.04.2	General Medieval History of Europe
S	☒	13.05.1	Central European History in General. ~~Reference Works & Bibliographies~~
S	☒	13.05.2	Central European History from the End of the Carolingian Empire to the Reformation
S	☒	13.06.0	Central European History from the Counter-Reformation to 1789
S	☒	13.07.0	Central European History from 1789 to 1918: Deutscher Bund & Deutsches Reich. The Austro-Hungarian Empire. Switzerland
S	☒	13.08.0	History of Germany, Austria, and Switzerland from 1918 to 1945
C	☒	13.08.1	Holocaust
S	☒	13.09.0	History of Germany, Austria, and Switzerland since 1945. Contemporary History C: DDR, former GDR

Approval Plan	Form Selection		
☐	☐	13.10.0	Special History of Individual German, Austrian, and Swiss Territories. Local History of the German Cultural Area
☐	☒	13.11.0	History of Scandinavia, including Finland
☐	☒	13.12.0	History of the British Isles & General Works on the Commonwealth of Nations
☐	☒	13.13.0	History of the Netherlands, Belgium & Luxembourg
R	☒	13.14.0	History of France
☐	☒	13.15.0	History of Italy, Spain, Portugal
☐	☒	13.16.0	History of Southeast Europe. The Balkan Countries. Greece
R	☒	13.17.0	History of Russia, the Soviet Union & the Successor States
R	☒	13.17.1	History of Poland, Hungary, Czechoslovakia & the Successor Republics
☐	☒	13.18.0	Modern Asian History *(starting with contact with the West)*
☐	☒	13.19.0	Modern African History *(starting with contact with the West)*
☐	☒	13.20.0	Modern History of Australia and the Pacific Area *(starting with contact with the West)*
☐	☒	13.21.0	Modern History of Central & South America *(starting with contact with the West)*
☐	☒	13.22.0	Modern History of North America *(starting with contact with the West)*
		14.	Manners & Customs, Folklore
☐	☐	14.01.0	Manners & Customs, Folklore in General. Reference Works & Bibliographies. Customs relating to Houses, Dwellings, Home, Family, Marriage, Private Life, Sex, Dress, Funeral Ceremonies, Festivals
☐	☐	14.02.0	Pastimes. Sports. Recreation. Games. Dance

40

HARRASSOWITZ

III. PROFILE NON-SUBJECT DESCRIPTORS

A. Geographical Definition

1. ☐ **German Approval Plan:**

   Publications of the German Cultural Areas (Germany, Austria, Switzerland)

   Language Specification
   ☐ No Restriction of Language
   ☐ English Language only
   ☐ German & English Language only

   ☐ Exclusions
   Please specify:

   Exhibition Catalogs
   The geographical coverage for Exhibition Catalogs is restricted to Germany, Austria, and Switzerland

   ☐ Include Exhibition Catalogs in all subjects
   ☐ Include Art Exhibition Catalogs only in the subject categories 4,5,9,11. *Submit more specific instructions with regard to 9 (pages 23-25)*
   ☐ Include Exhibition Catalogs only from subject categories other than Fine Arts (i.e. History, Literature, Science, etc.)
   ☐ Exclude all Exhibition Catalogs
   ☐ Other exclusions or inclusions
   Please specify:

2. ☐ **Continental European English Language Plan:**

   Original English Language Publications from the Continental European Countries covered by our program currently (The Netherlands, Belgium, Denmark, Sweden, Hungary, Poland, France)

3. ☐ **Any Special Geographical Restrictions:**
   Please specify:

B. Starting Point

A Form Selection Program can be started at any time. For an Approval Plan we suggest to begin with a new imprint year
Please note your instructions:

C. Level of Selection Emphasis (For Books only - Forms are always comprehensive)

The level of selection emphasis for all subjects covered by the approval plan should be:

☐ Comprehensive (C)
☐ Selective (S)
☐ Representative (R)
☐ The level of selection emphasis differs from subject to subject. Please annotate in the Subject Outline by using the codes C, S, or R.

D. Price Limit

1. The Approval Plan selection is usually restricted to titles costing less than $100.00 or $150.00 per volume depending on the library's decision. Any realistic price limit can be accommodated. More expensive titles are announced on our forms.

2. The Form Selection Program, of course, covers all pertinent titles, regardless of price.

3. For your approval plan, please indicate your price limit per volume: _____

I. Majors Scientific Books, Inc.

MAJORS APPROVAL PLAN
EXCEPTION TABLE PROFILE

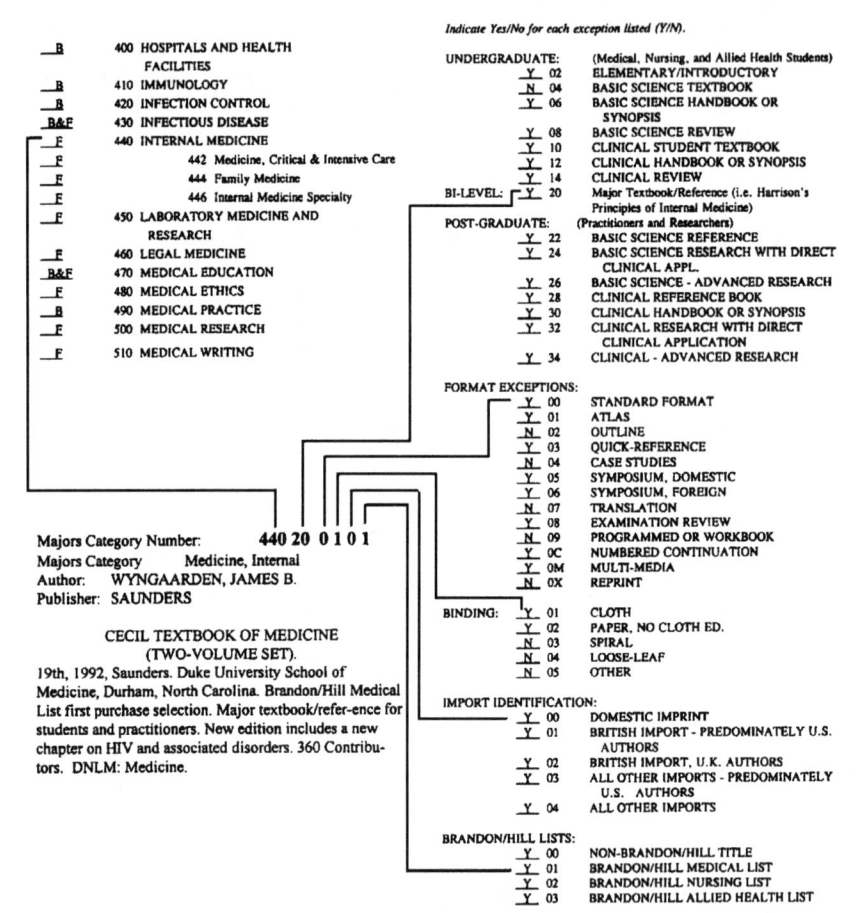

Indicate Yes/No for each exception listed (Y/N).

_B_	400	HOSPITALS AND HEALTH FACILITIES			
_B_	410	IMMUNOLOGY			
_B_	420	INFECTION CONTROL			
_B&F_	430	INFECTIOUS DISEASE			
_F_	440	INTERNAL MEDICINE			
_F_		442 Medicine, Critical & Intensive Care			
_F_		444 Family Medicine			
_F_		446 Internal Medicine Specialty			
_F_	450	LABORATORY MEDICINE AND RESEARCH			
_F_	460	LEGAL MEDICINE			
_B&F_	470	MEDICAL EDUCATION			
_F_	480	MEDICAL ETHICS			
_B_	490	MEDICAL PRACTICE			
_F_	500	MEDICAL RESEARCH			
_F_	510	MEDICAL WRITING			

UNDERGRADUATE: (Medical, Nursing, and Allied Health Students)
- _Y_ 02 ELEMENTARY/INTRODUCTORY
- _N_ 04 BASIC SCIENCE TEXTBOOK
- _Y_ 06 BASIC SCIENCE HANDBOOK OR SYNOPSIS
- _Y_ 08 BASIC SCIENCE REVIEW
- _Y_ 10 CLINICAL STUDENT TEXTBOOK
- _Y_ 12 CLINICAL HANDBOOK OR SYNOPSIS
- _Y_ 14 CLINICAL REVIEW

BI-LEVEL: _Y_ 20 Major Textbook/Reference (i.e. Harrison's Principles of Internal Medicine)

POST-GRADUATE: (Practitioners and Researchers)
- _Y_ 22 BASIC SCIENCE REFERENCE
- _Y_ 24 BASIC SCIENCE RESEARCH WITH DIRECT CLINICAL APPL.
- _Y_ 26 BASIC SCIENCE - ADVANCED RESEARCH
- _Y_ 28 CLINICAL REFERENCE BOOK
- _Y_ 30 CLINICAL HANDBOOK OR SYNOPSIS
- _Y_ 32 CLINICAL RESEARCH WITH DIRECT CLINICAL APPLICATION
- _Y_ 34 CLINICAL - ADVANCED RESEARCH

FORMAT EXCEPTIONS:
- _Y_ 00 STANDARD FORMAT
- _Y_ 01 ATLAS
- _N_ 02 OUTLINE
- _Y_ 03 QUICK-REFERENCE
- _N_ 04 CASE STUDIES
- _Y_ 05 SYMPOSIUM, DOMESTIC
- _Y_ 06 SYMPOSIUM, FOREIGN
- _N_ 07 TRANSLATION
- _Y_ 08 EXAMINATION REVIEW
- _N_ 09 PROGRAMMED OR WORKBOOK
- _Y_ 0C NUMBERED CONTINUATION
- _Y_ 0M MULTI-MEDIA
- _N_ 0X REPRINT

Majors Category Number: **440 20 0 1 0 1**
Majors Category: Medicine, Internal
Author: WYNGAARDEN, JAMES B.
Publisher: SAUNDERS

CECIL TEXTBOOK OF MEDICINE
(TWO-VOLUME SET).
19th, 1992, Saunders. Duke University School of Medicine, Durham, North Carolina. Brandon/Hill Medical List first purchase selection. Major textbook/refer-ence for students and practitioners. New edition includes a new chapter on HIV and associated disorders. 360 Contributors. DNLM: Medicine.

BINDING:
- _Y_ 01 CLOTH
- _Y_ 02 PAPER, NO CLOTH ED.
- _N_ 03 SPIRAL
- _N_ 04 LOOSE-LEAF
- _N_ 05 OTHER

IMPORT IDENTIFICATION:
- _Y_ 00 DOMESTIC IMPRINT
- _Y_ 01 BRITISH IMPORT - PREDOMINATELY U.S. AUTHORS
- _Y_ 02 BRITISH IMPORT, U.K. AUTHORS
- _Y_ 03 ALL OTHER IMPORTS - PREDOMINATELY U.S. AUTHORS
- _Y_ 04 ALL OTHER IMPORTS

BRANDON/HILL LISTS:
- _Y_ 00 NON-BRANDON/HILL TITLE
- _Y_ 01 BRANDON/HILL MEDICAL LIST
- _Y_ 02 BRANDON/HILL NURSING LIST
- _Y_ 03 BRANDON/HILL ALLIED HEALTH LIST

J. Aux Amateurs de Livres

**APPROVAL PLAN
and SLIPS SERVICE**
DEWEY CLASSES

Language and Literature Approval Plan Profile for Sample University

The Approval Plan is intended to acquire new scholarly works and literary criticism published in the French language. We want to spend at least $8,000. but no more than $9,000. The primary areas of interest for the automatic shipment of materials are works:
 1. By or about the authors who appear on the attached French authors list 2. By authors the AAL selectors believe to have potential literary merit.

General Instructions:
1. The Plan is to begin with works published in April 1998.
2. Ignore a firm order if it is placed for a title sent on approval unless the firm order indicates it is for a duplicate or replacement copy. 3. Send titles in series but do not duplicate titles we have on standing order. 4. All packages, invoices and correspondence should be sent to Monograph Acquisitions. Sample University, 35 W. 14th Street, City, State 48176.

Send as a slip rather than a book if the individual publication: 1. Cost more than $75. 2. May not be returned 3. Is a reprint 4. Revised editions unless they contain substantial additional material or textual changes. 5. Is a textbook 6. Was first published in another language

Notes

1. Hunter L. Kevil, "The Approval Plan of Smaller Scope," *Library Acquisitions: Practice & Theory* 9(1): 20 (1985).
2. Ann L. O'Neill, "How the Richard Abel Co., Inc. Changed the Way We Work," *Library Acquisitions: Practice & Theory* 17(1): 42 (1993).
3. Ibid, 41.
4. Ibid, 42.
5. Association of Research Libraries, Office of Management Studies, *Approval Plans,* SPEC Kit, no. 141 (Washington, D.C.: ARL, 1988), 11.
6. Frances C. Wilkinson and Connie Capers Thorson, "The RFP Process: Rational, Educational, Necessary or There Ain't No Such Thing as a Free Lunch," *Library Acquisitions: Practice & Theory* 19(2): 263 (1995).
7. Edward J. Lockman, "A Perspective on Library Book Gathering Plans," in *Technical Services Today and Tomorrow* (Englewood, Colo.: Libraries Unlimited, 1990), 17.
8. Mary Eldredge, "Major Issues in Approval Plans: The Case for Active Management," *Acquisitions Librarian* 16 (1996): 53.
9. Amy E. Arnold, "Approval Slips and Faculty Participation in Book Selection in a Small University Library," *Collection Management* 18(1/2): 98–99 (1993).
10. Judy Quinn, "The New Approval Plans: Surrendering to the Vendor . . . or in the Driver's Seat?" *Library Journal* 116(15): 38–41 (1991).
11. Association for Library Collections & Technical Services, Publications Committee, Foreign Book Dealers Directories Series Subcommittee, *Foreign Book and Serial Vendors Directories* (Chicago: Association for Library Collections & Technical Services, American Library Association), 1996– .
12. Anthony W. Ferguson, "British Approval Plan Books: American or British Vendor?" *Collection Building* 8(4): 18–22 (1988).
13. Betsy Kruger, "U.K. Books and Their U.S. Imprints: A Cost and Duplication Study," *Library Acquisitions: Practice & Theory* 15(3): 304 (1991).
14. Mary Eldredge, "United Kingdom Approval Plans and United States Academic Libraries: Are They Necessary and Cost Effective?" *Library Acquisitions: Practice & Theory* 18(2): 173 (1994).

15. Joan Grant, "Approval Plans: The Vendor as Preselector," in *Understanding the Business of Library Acquisitions,* ed. Karen A. Schmidt (Chicago: American Library Association, 1990), 161–62.

16. John H. Reidelbach and Gary M. Shirk, "Selecting an Approval Plan Vendor: A Step-by-Step Process," *Library Acquisitions: Practice & Theory* 7(2): 116 (1983).

17. Wilkinson and Thorson, "The RFP Process," 251.

18. Wilkinson and Thorson, "The RFP Process," 259–60.

19. R. Charles Wittenberg, "The Approval Plan: An Idea Whose Time Has Gone? and Come Again?" *Library Acquisitions: Practice & Theory* 12(2): 241 (1988).

20. Jennifer S. Cargill and Brian Alley, *Practical Approval Plan Management* (Phoenix: Oryx Press, 1979), 34–41.

21. Wilkinson and Thorson, "The RFP Process," 251–68.

22. Katina Strauch and Heather Miller, "Cloth over Paper or Paper over Cloth—Up to You," *Against the Grain* 5(3): 10 (1993).

23. Dana L. Alessi, "Coping with Library Needs: The Approval Vendor's Response/Responsibility," in *Issues in Acquisitions: Programs and Evaluation,* ed. Sul H. Lee (Ann Arbor, Mich.: Pierian Press, 1984), 97; Robert F. Nardini, "The Approval Plan Profiling Session," *Library Acquisitions: Practice & Theory* 18(3): 289–95 (1994).

24. Steven M. Rouzer, "Acquiring Monographic Series by Approval Plan: Is the Standing Order Obsolescent?" *Library Acquisitions: Practice & Theory* 19(4): 395 (1995).

25. Rosann Bazirjian, "The Impact of Approval Plans on Acquisitions Operations and Work Flow," *The Acquisitions Librarian* 16 (1996): 32.

26. Mary Eldredge, "Major Issues in Approval Plans," 57.

27. Douglas Duchin, "The Role of Suppliers: A North American Perspective," in *Collection Management in Academic Libraries,* ed. Clare Jenkins and Mary Morley (Aldershot, Eng.: Gower, 1991), 135.

28. Grant, "Approval Plans," 153–64; Wilkinson and Thorson, "The RFP Process."

29. Kay Womack, Agnes Adams, Judy L. Johnson, et al., "An Approval Plan Review," *Library Acquisitions: Practice & Theory* 12(3/4): 363–78 (1988).

30. Beau David Chase, "Approval Plan Evaluation Studies: A Selected Annotated Bibliography, 1969–1996," *Against the Grain* 8(4): 18–24 (1996).

31. William J. Hook, "Approval Plans for Religious and Theological Libraries," *Library Acquisitions: Practice & Theory* 15(2): 215–27 (1991).

32. Glorianna St. Clair and Jane Treadwell, "Science and Technology Approval Plans Compared," *Library Resources & Technical Services* 33(4): 391 (1989).

33. Mary Eldredge, "Major Issues in Approval Plans," 53.

34. Martin Warzala, "Evolution of Approval Services," *Library Trends* 42(3): 522 (1994).

35. Lynne C. Branche Brown, "An Expert System for Predicting Approval Plan Receipts," *Library Acquisitions: Practice & Theory* 17(2): 155–64 (1993).

36. Meredith L. Smith, "Return to Sender? Analyzing Approval Plan Returns," *The Acquisitions Librarian* 16 (1996), 47.

37. Marion Wilden-Hart, "The Long-Term Effects of Approval Plans," *Library Resources & Technical Services* 14(3): 403–4 (1970).

38. Robert F. Nardini, Charles M. Getchell Jr., and Thomas E. Cheever, "Approval Plan Overlap: A Study of Four Libraries," *The Acquisitions Librarian* 16 (1996), 75–97.

Glossary

Note: Some definitions of other approval-type plans are included here because they are discussed in articles on the evolution of approval plans, even though they are not included in the text of this *Guide*.

academic level   A term used for a group of *non-subject parameters* that describe the intended or estimated level of scholarship of a title.

approval plan   Arrangement with a publisher or with a vendor to send materials automatically. It is not necessary for the library to order title by title. Titles that are not considered appropriate may be returned by the library. An approval plan with a vendor is usually an agreement that the library will receive current imprints selected for the library on the basis of a detailed *profile*.

bibliographic form   A multipart form that is supplied with each book in an approval shipment. It contains basic bibliographic information, as well as price, broad subject category, academic level, and other descriptive information. This same information in the database is used for the vendor's notification service of new titles.

blanket orders   In contrast with approval plans, blanket orders do not generally allow return privileges with simple deductions from the invoice. Blanket orders can be arranged with publishers or distributors of non-print materials or vendors. With blanket orders, quality is less important than comprehensiveness of coverage. Blanket orders can be as narrow as a specific publisher's series or as broad as a request to send all material of a particular type or subject. A common blanket order is for all materials, or a specified subset, published by an association.

deposit accounts   An option that allows approval customers to pay all or a portion of the estimated annual billing in advance. Depending on the amount prepaid, the typical discount is from 1.5 percent to 4.5 percent more than a regular plan, where invoices are paid after the receipt of titles.

EDI (Electronic Data Interchange)   The exchange of routine business transactions in a computer-processable format.

Farmington Plan   Developed out of a concern for the interruptions in collection development that occurred during World War II, the Farmington Plan (1948–1972) sought to ensure that at least one copy of every book that was important for research, regardless of where it was published, would be available in at least one American library. Libraries in the plan chose a subject area and agreed to accept shipments in those areas. Foreign dealers gained experience in selecting for American libraries which later transferred to their approval plans.

gathering plan This term was used interchangeably with "approval plan" in the early history of the approval plan concept, but today it is usually used to refer to an agreement with a foreign vendor to gather and ship material of a specified type or subject.

geographic designator A term applied to a group of *non-subject parameters* that represent major geographic areas.

Greenaway Plan Emerson Greenaway, former director of the Free Library of Philadelphia, began a plan in 1958 in which publishers sent copies of all of their trade books to a library at the same time that they sent out copies for review, usually before publication. Discounts were high and returns were not allowed. Large public libraries found this plan attractive because it allowed for review, with book in hand, early enough to order multiple copies to meet popular demand and to satisfy branches.

Latin American Cooperative Acquisition Project (LACAP) A plan in which Stechert-Hafner, Inc., employed agents throughout Latin America to gather and ship publications to American libraries that had blanket order agreements. During the time of its existence, from 1960 to 1973, a number of Latin American dealers gained experience with blanket orders for U.S. libraries.

management reports Reports of approval sales and returns, which are often issued quarterly, arrange data by subject code or LC class to indicate the number of titles and prices in each category. Reports can be used to determine the average price and expenditure by subject, as well as the number of titles provided, accepted, and returned by subject.

modifier See *non-subject parameter*

non-subject parameter (NSP) A term used to describe a title in ways other than by subject, such as price or whether or not a title is a reprint. It may be used to describe the intended audience, such as juvenile or popular. It can convey scholarly content, a textual format like workbook or textbook, or a physical format. Non-subject parameters can be used to block a series for which the library already has a standing order. There is no standardization of non-subject parameters among book vendors. Time and effort are required to define the non-subject parameters in a profile to the library's satisfaction.

notification slips or forms Also called selection slips or announcement slips, notification slips amount to a current awareness service for new publications. Multi-part forms are sent for titles that match a library's *profile*.

This service can be used in place of receiving titles on approval. Titles ordered from slips have the same return privileges as firm orders. Some libraries use slips to supplement an approval plan—receiving titles under a basic profile and slips for titles which fall outside of that profile, such as those which cost more than the price limit or are textbooks, etc. A library may want to use slips to monitor the output of a publisher. Slips are always sent when a publisher refuses to accept returns.

PL-480 Under the provisions of this law, foreign vendors gained experience with the blanket order concept. Foreign currencies, which were obtained by the U.S. government through the sale of agricultural products, were spent on books, journals, and newspapers instead of exchanging them for U.S. dollars. Initiated for the Library of Congress, other libraries also participated if they agreed to accept, retain, and service whatever was sent to them.

profile What the library wishes to collect, expressed in codes that can be read by a computer and that form a set of instructions to the vendor about what to send and what to withhold. Vendor-specific terms and numbering schemes are used. Profiles may be divided into sub-profiles.

publisher-based plans Some libraries opt for a publisher-based plan as opposed to a subject-based plan. Some common publisher-based plans are for university presses, small presses, or major commercial presses. Subject-based and publisher-based plans can be combined when a subject-based plan is limited to a group of named publishers. Some publishers offer approval plans of their own. Because extensive analysis of the subject content is not necessary, vendor processing of titles is faster than it is for a subject-based plan.

retrospective collection development The coded titles in an approval vendor's database are used to identify and obtain older imprints for a new academic program or for a collection enhancement undertaken as a result of an unexpected fiscal windfall or for a major development effort. If the library's collection is in machine-readable format, the resulting list can be matched electronically against a library's holdings. Otherwise, lists or forms are printed for manual checking. Out-of-print titles can be identified.

review shelves An area used to display titles that have been received on approval. Many libraries screen for duplication or error before the titles are arranged in subject order. Ordinarily, selectors (faculty or librarians) have one week to examine approval titles.

standing order An order placed with a vendor or the publisher directly for all publications in a series, all volumes of a set, or all publications of a single publisher.

subject-analysis Titles coded so that they can be matched by a computer against the subjects on a library's profiles. Subject analysis can occur at the point of initial identification of a publisher's proposed title, or with the book in hand, or at both points, with greater refinement at the second stage.

subject-based plan The subject-based plan may be the most common type of plan. It can cover any number of the subjects found in library materials. The library selects coverage from the hierarchy of subjects in a vendor's thesaurus and then defines the *non-subject parameters*.

subject-descriptor Terms used to represent an area of knowledge.

subject thesaurus Subject descriptors arranged in hierarchical order by LC classification or in a vendor-developed outline. This arrangement allows libraries to receive all or part of a subject. A subject thesaurus can also be arranged alphabetically.

type of material Approval plans have been developed based on the type of material, such as music scores, art exhibition catalogs, non-print media, children's titles, and best-sellers. These plans may be further defined by publisher and *non-subject parameters*.

X12 Accredited Standards Committee X12 of the American National Standards Institute (ANSI) charged with developing standards that specify the format and data content of electronic business transactions. X12 refers to the standards developed by this committee.

Selected Bibliography

Introductory Reading

Abel, Richard. "The Origin of the Library Approval Plan." *Publishing Research Quarterly* 11(1): 46–56 (1995).

O'Neill, Ann L. "How the Richard Abel Co., Inc. Changed the Way We Work." *Library Acquisitions: Practice & Theory* 17(1): 41–46 (1993).

Rossi, Gary J. "Library Approval Plans: A Selected Annotated Bibliography." *Library Acquisitions: Practice & Theory* 11(1): 3–34 (1987).

Approval Plan Management

Alessi, Dana L. "Coping with Library Needs: The Approval Vendor's Response/Responsibility." In *Issues in Acquisitions: Programs & Evaluation,* edited by Sul H. Lee, 91–109. Ann Arbor, Mich.: Pierian Press, 1984.

Bucknall, Carolyn. "Mass Buying Programs." In *Collection Management: A New Treatise,* edited by Charles B. Osburn and Ross Atkinson, 337–49. Foundations in Library and Information Science, vol. 26B. Greenwich, Conn.: JAI Press, 1991.

Cargill, Jennifer S. and Brian Alley. *Practical Approval Plan Management.* Phoenix, Ariz.: Oryx Press, 1979.

Duchin, Douglas. "The Role of Suppliers: A North American Perspective." In *Collection Management in Academic Libraries,* edited by Clare Jenkins and Mary Morley, 119–38. Aldershot, England: Gower, 1991.

Grant, Joan. "Approval Plans: The Vendor as Preselector." In *Understanding the Business of Library Acquisitions,* edited by Karen A. Schmidt, 153–64. Chicago: American Library Association, 1990.

Lockman, Edward J. "A Perspective on Library Book Gathering Plans." In *Technical Services Today and Tomorrow,* edited by Michael Gorman, 15–21. Englewood, Colo.: Libraries Unlimited, 1990.

Miller, Heather S. "Approval Plans." In *Managing Acquisitions and Vendor Relations,* 69–81. How-to-Do-It Manuals for Libraries, no. 23. New York: Neal-Schuman, 1992.

Nardini, Robert F. "The Approval Plan Profiling Session." *Library Acquisitions: Practice & Theory* 18(3): 289–95 (1994).

———. "Approval Plans: Politics and Performance." *College & Research Libraries* 54(5): 417–25 (1993).

Rouzer, Steven M. "Acquiring Monographic Series by Approval Plan: Is the Standing Order Obsolescent?" *Library Acquisitions: Practice & Theory* 19(4): 395–401 (1995).

Sandy, John H., ed. *Approval Plans: Issues and Innovations.* The Acquisitions Librarian, no. 16. Binghamton, N.Y.: Haworth Press, 1996.

General

Association of Research Libraries, Office of Management Studies. *Approval Plans.* Spec Kit, no. 141. Washington, D.C.: ARL, 1988.

Association of Research Libraries, Office of Management Services. *Evolution and Status of Approval Plans.* Spec Kit, no. 221. Washington, D.C.: ARL, 1997.

Spyers-Duran, Peter and Thomas Mann Jr., eds. *Shaping Library Collections for the 1980s.* Phoenix, Ariz.: Oryx Press, 1980.

Vendor Evaluation

Barker, Joseph. "Vendor Studies Redux: Evaluating the Approval Plan Option from Within." *Library Acquisitions: Practice & Theory* 13(2): 133–41 (1989).

Reidelbach, John H. and Gary M. Shirk. "Selecting an Approval Plan Vendor: A Step-by-Step Process." *Library Acquisitions: Practice & Theory* 7(2): 115–22 (1983).

———. "Selecting an Approval Plan Vendor II: Comparative Vendor Data." *Library Acquisitions: Practice & Theory* 8(3): 157–202 (1984).

———. "Selecting an Approval Plan Vendor III: Academic Librarians' Evaluations of Eight United States Approval Plan Vendors." *Library Acquisitions: Practice & Theory* 9(3): 177–260 (1985).

Wilkinson, Frances C. and Connie Capers Thorson. "The RFP Process: Rational, Educational, Necessary or There Ain't No Such Thing as a Free Lunch." *Library Acquisitions: Practice & Theory* 19(2): 251–68 (1995).

Womack, Kay, Agnes Adams, Judy L. Johnson, and Katherine L. Walter. "An Approval Plan Review: The Organization and Process." *Library Acquisitions: Practice & Theory* 12(3/4): 363–78 (1988).

Foreign Vendors

Association for Library Collections & Technical Services, Publications Committee, Foreign Book Dealers Directories Series Subcommittee. *Foreign Book and Serial Vendors Directories.* Chicago: Association for Library Collections & Technical Services, American Library Association, 1996–

British Approval Plans

Eldredge, Mary. "United Kingdom Approval Plans and United States Academic Libraries: Are They Necessary and Cost Effective?" *Library Acquisitions: Practice & Theory* 18(2): 165–78 (1994).

Ferguson, Anthony W. "British Approval Plan Books: American or British Vendor?" *Collection Building* 8(4): 18–22 (1988).

Kruger, Betsy. "U.K. Books and Their U.S. Imprints: A Cost and Duplication Study." *Library Acquisitions: Practice & Theory* 15(3): 301–12 (1991).

Special Applications

Arnold, Amy E. "Approval Slips and Faculty Participation in Book Selection in a Small University Library." *Collection Management* 18(1/2): 89–102 (1993).

Dole, Wanda V. "The Feasibility of Approval Plans for Small College Libraries." In *Collection Development in College Libraries,* edited by Joanne Schneider Hill, William E. Hannaford Jr., and Ronald H. Epp, 154–62. Chicago: American Library Association, 1991.

Hook, William J. "Approval Plans for Religious and Theological Libraries." *Library Acquisitions: Practice & Theory* 15(2): 215–27 (1991).

Kaatrude, Peter B. "Approval Plan versus Conventional Selection: Determining the Overlap." *Collection Management* 11(1/2): 145–50 (1989).

Kevil, L. Hunter. "The Approval Plan of Smaller Scope." *Library Acquisitions: Practice & Theory* 9(1): 13–20 (1985).

Quinn, Judy. "The New Approval Plans: Surrendering to the Vendor . . . or in the Driver's Seat?" *Library Journal* 116(15): 38–41 (1991).

St. Clair, Glorianna and Jane Treadwell. "Science and Technology Approval Plans Compared." *Library Resources & Technical Services* 33(4): 382–92 (1989).

Future Applications

Brown, Lynne C. Branche. "An Expert System for Predicting Approval Plan Receipts." *Library Acquisitions: Practice & Theory* 17(2): 155–64 (1993).

Bush, Carmel C., Margo Sassé, and Patricia Smith. "Toward a New World Order: A Survey of Outsourcing Capabilities of Vendors for Acquisitions, Cataloging and Collection Development Services." *Library Acquisitions: Practice & Theory* 18(4): 397–416 (1994).

Warzala, Martin. "Evolution of Approval Services." *Library Trends* 42(3): 514–23 (1994).

Wilden-Hart, Marion. "The Long-Term Effects of Approval Plans." *Library Resources & Technical Services* 14(3): 400–406 (1970).

Index

Abel, Richard, 2
Academic level, 43
Academic libraries, 16, 24
Accounting, 16, 24
Acquisitions, 4, 6, 14, 15, 16, 17
Approval plan, 1, 3, 48
   British, 8
   foreign, 2, 7, 8, 17, 19, 20, 23
   publisher-based, 2, 15, 45
   shelf-ready books, 3, 12
   subject-based, 1, 15, 51
   type of material, 2, 7, 51
Authority records, 11

Blanket orders, 48
Budget, 13, 16, 21–23

Cataloging records, 3, 11, 14, 17
Collection development
   collection development policy, 1, 5, 14, 16
   retrospective, 7, 19–20, 45
Collection management, 1, 4, 5, 6, 14, 16, 18, 21–23
Contract, 13
Curriculum, 16, 21

Deposit, 4, 10, 48
Discount, 4, 5, 9, 10, 13, 17, 23
Display, 18

EDI, 4, 48
Encumbrances, 13

Faculty, 5, 14, 15, 21, 24
Farmington Plan, 48–49

Firm orders, 13, 18, 19, 24–25
Forms
   bibliographic, 2–3, 10, 48

Gathering plan, 49
Geographic designator, 49
Greenaway Plan, 49

History, 2–3

Invoice, 10, 14
   electronic, 4, 11, 14

Latin American Cooperative Acquisition Project (LACAP), 49

Management, 4, 5, 6, 20, 23
management reports, 6, 9, 12, 22, 49

Non-subject parameter, 2, 14, 15, 16, 22, 49
Notification slips, 6, 9, 12–13, 17, 20, 23, 49–50

Outsourcing, 11, 12

Paperbacks, 15
PL-480, 45
Politics, 22
Profile, 1, 9, 10, 11, 15, 16, 21–22, 24–25, 50
   design, 8, 9, 14–15, 22, 24–25
   monitoring, 12, 22, 24–25
Public libraries, 6–7, 19, 24
Publishers, 22, 25

Returns, 4–6, 9, 17, 18–19, 22–23
Review, 7, 18, 19
   review shelves, 50

Self-credit, 10
Shipping, 10, 15
Societies, 17, 22, 25
Standing orders, 17, 19, 50
Subject-analysis, 22–23, 50–51
Subject-descriptor, 51
Subject thesaurus, 51

Thesaurus, 15
Thor Power Tool Company, 6
Type of material, 51

Vendors, 5, 11, 13, 16, 19, 23, 24, 25
   changing, 8
   contacting, 8, 9
   evaluating, 9, 10, 20–21

X12, 4, 51

FOR USE IN LIBRARY ONLY

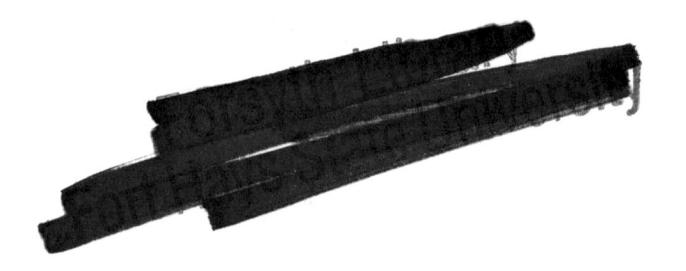